Southern Sudan
The Foundation of a War Economy

George Tombe Lako

Southern Sudan

The Foundation of a War Economy

Peter Lang
Europäischer Verlag der Wissenschaften

Die Deutsche Bibliothek - CIP-Einheitsaufnahme

Lako, George Tombe:

Southern Sudan : the foundation of a war economy / George Tombe Lako. - Frankfurt am Main ; Berlin ; Bern ; New York ; Paris ; Wien : Lang, 1993
ISBN 3-631-46579-3

ISBN 3-631-46579-3

Table of Contents

List of Tables, Maps and Diagrams

TABLES

MAPS

Preface

Specific studies of the economic development of Southern Sudan are hard to find. Only brief references to it are available in the Economic Surveys, the National Plans of the Ministry of Finance in Khartoum and a few other publications. Therefore, it is imperative to provide a review/discussion of the state of this economy because, when the present war inevitably ends, development has to be revived. Much will need rebuilding.

To rebuild means that policy makers and planners need to have a thorough knowledge of past socio-economic structures and the main features of the economy, its constraints and limitations. Quite often politicians and technocrats laud the vast natural resources of Southern Sudan and formulate their plans or projects on that basis only. Though it is true, and perhaps it is a necessary premise to begin from, it is certainly insufficient for planning, if we are to avoid the false starts Third World countries are so prone to, Southern Sudan included.

Policy makers in Southern Sudan will face difficult challenges in agriculture, the backbone of the economy in the whole country and of course the South. Programmes of social and economic reconstruction and rehabilitation will obviously have to begin from wherever or whatever the war will have left intact.

This book deals with the subject of economic development in Southern Sudan (most of the material for it is based on the first chapters of the author's Ph.D. thesis) and the war impact on it (based on data more recently collected in the South); but basically it aims to fill a gap in our knowledge of that economy. It is divided into six chapters covering the pre-independence and the post-independence periods, each is examined separately more for the convenience of the analysis rather than because some major economic transformation has taken place. Perhaps the division will help us to perceive some of the ways in which economic development has taken place during the two periods.

During the pre-independence period (i.e. before 1956), which is discussed in chapter 2, most of the population engaged in agriculture/animal husbandry, or just one or the other activity. The economy was mostly non-monetary. Some of the tribes, such as the Dinka, led a predominantly pastoral life, although the economic reliance of these peoples on livestock products is much less than was often supposed. At the other extreme the Zande, and other smaller tribes, lived in forested and tsetse infested parts of the Equatorial Region, owned hardly any livestock and relied almost entirely on crop production.

Chapter 3, covers the post-1956 independence period. Although the main features of the economy have remained largely the same as before independence, some changes are discernible: and, particularly since the 1972 Peace Accord, efforts have been made to improve on general economic development. Chapter 4 discusses the position of the South within the Sudan economy. Chapter 5 is an analysis of the then prevailing development policy epitomised in the Six Year Plan (1977/78–1982/83) that ended abruptly due to the emergence of the current war in May 1985. Chapter 6 examines the impact of the current war on the economy. Chapter 7, taking Equatoria region as an example, is in a way a summary or a bird's eye view of the present state of the economy of Southern Sudan as a whole.

George Tombe Lako
Nairobi, March 1993

Map 1. Southern Sudan

Source: Johnson, Douglas H., The Southern Sudan, p. 3, Minority Rights Group, Report No. 78.

Chapter 1

Historical Background

There is a vast literature on the history of the Sudan. So this chapter simply aims to provide a brief history which selects for attention only those events and developments in the interrelationships between Britain, Egypt and the Sudan which have affected the present phase of economic and socio-political development in the Southern Sudan.

The first two sections describe the land and the basic manpower and population characteristics. The third is an account of the history of the Southern Sudan during the Turco-Egyptian and Mahdiya eras, and highlights the gradual opening up of the area to the outside world and the subsequent trade in slaves. The chapter ends with an analysis of the aims of the British and the reactions of Southern Sudanese to their rule.

The Land

Sudan is the largest country in Africa, with an area of 2.5 million square kilometres and, according to the 1983 census, a population of 21,592 millions. The same source reveals that 69 percent of the population live in the rural areas, 11 percent as nomads and 20 percent are urban based. However, the present war, which began in 1983, and the 1983–1985 famine modified population distribution: 4 million peasants and pastoralists left their villages to join the urban poor or live in appalling conditions in the outskirts of the large urban centres. Although one third of the country is desert and semi-desert, it has an estimated 200 mn. acres of cultivable and pasture land.

The Southern Sudan, or Southern Region (defunct since the redivision of 1983), or Southern Regions (comprising Equatoria, Bahr el Ghazal and Upper Nile) as they are now called, is roughly one-third (approximately 650,000 square kilometres) of the total area of the Sudan. Each of the present three regions has a status equal to that of each of the six regions established in the North in 1980/81.[1]

There are three distinct physical areas (see Map of Southern Sudan): the broad alluvial plains of the Upper Nile Basin, in the north-east and extending westwards up to the land of the Ngok Dinka between Bahr el Ghazal and Southern Kordofan provinces; the iron-stone plateau, running north-west to south-east; and the southern-most part which consists of mountain ranges rising to several thousand metres.

The alluvial plains of the Upper Nile Basin cover about half of the South, are extremely flat and have fairly heavy rainfall (approximately 900 mm per year). Rainfall and river flooding combine to create the vast swamps and vegetation which give rise to the characteristic system of land use in this region. It is here that the Nilotes, particularly the Dinka, practice their transhuman semi-nomadic way of life. The iron-stone plateau and the mountainous region in the far south differ from the clay plains physically and climatically. There are more rivers here and the drainage is better. The soils are lateritic and leaching and erosion reduce fertility quite drastically so that the soils in the clay plains can be regarded as more fertile than those in these areas. Rainfall is heavier than in the clay plains (approximately 1,000–1,500 mm per year) and also lasts longer, often up to six to eight months in parts, particularly in areas around high mountains or the tropical forests of Western Equatoria. In general, the vegetation is high rainfall savannah woodland, with many varieties of trees and grass. Unlike in the clay plains, subsistence farming is predominantly based on shifting cultivation, although some tribes in the south-east, like the Toposa, Turkana and Didinga, depend more on cattle rearing.

Population and Manpower

The preliminary data of the 1973 census, gave an unexpectedly low estimate of 2.8 million for the population of the Southern Region. This was raised to 2.9 million, to allow for under-enumeration, but was still low, because a minimum of 375,000 persons was omitted, i.e. refugees living abroad and people then hiding in the forests, still uncertain about the Peace signed in Addis Ababa in 1972. "While projections of the census figures give a population figure of 3,077,000 people for the Southern Region, it is believed that a more realistic figure would be at least 3,570,000 and, more probably, a figure of nearer 4 million should be considered".[2] In the absence of a more recent census, both Government and UN bodies now float the figure of 7 million as more realistic since that for the whole country is now estimated to be 22 million.

In the 1950s and 1960s, many Southerners migrated to the North because of the civil war and also in search of jobs in the Gezira Scheme and the industrial complexes of the Three Towns (Khartoum, Khartoum North and Omdurman). Others preferred to hide in the bush, particularly in areas of dense forests or savannah woodlands. Others, like the Nuer and Dinka, whose land is flat and mainly savannah grassland, moved to safer areas in the North. Of course, some Southerners, especially the young and able-bodied, joined the 'freedom fighters' (Anyanya) and a substantial number took refuge in neighbouring countries (e.g. Uganda, Kenya, Zaire and Ethiopia). The end of the civil war meant that these last groups could return to their homes.

However, the present war has caused an unprecedented mass movement of Southerners away from their rural and even their urban settings. The Government estimates that there are at present over 2 million displaced Southerners in Khartoum living in shanties in such parts as Fatihab, Shejera, Hag Yusuf, Mayo, etc. An unknown, but equally large number, are squatting in towns in the Gezira Scheme, Gedaref, Kordofan and Darfur. The populations of the southern towns such as Juba, Wau and Malakal have swelled due to the presence of large numbers of rural-displaced persons seeking food and security which they had lost in their homelands because of the war between the SPLA (Sudan Peoples Liberation Army) of Col. John Garang and the national army.

Another group of displaced Southerners are in the bush either alone or under the umbrella of the SPLA, but their numbers are not known. Precise numbers of refugees in Uganda, Ethiopia, Zaire and Kenya are hard to determine since the populations in camps varies according to the intensity of the war across the borders. But most observers believe Southern refugees could number well over a million.

The last civil war (1955–1972) and the present one are having drastic effects on population growth within the South. In general, the 1955–56 census showed that the South had some of the highest birth rates in the country, with Bahr el Ghazal at the top. However, seventeen years of hostilities have meant that not only were lives lost in the cross-fire between the Anyanya and Government troops, but also many people died from hunger and disease, since most economic and social development had come to a standstill. After the 1972 Peace Accord the rate of population increase was expected to rise substantially above the projected annual natural rate of increase of 1.7 percent. But the present war must be offsetting this greatly.

The 1973 census indicated that the South had an overall crude economic activity rate of 30 percent. However, as pointed out in Mills' (1976) study (which is the only one on the subject), a figure of 87 percent economically active population is more realistic if we include female employment and estimate that the range of working life is from 10 or less to 60 years or above. Mills also concluded that, in general, the population of the South shows a normal distribution as regards age and sex. Both men and women participate in agriculture, animal husbandry, etc. from childhood onwards.

The economy of the South is still heavily dependent on subsistence agriculture and/or animal husbandry. The 1973 census figures seemed to suggest a change in sectoral balance as greater numbers were recorded in secondary and tertiary activities. This was largely explained by the large numbers of unemployed in such secondary activities as construction and by the growing civil service and administration. Not surprisingly, the 1973 census data showed that over three-quarters of the population depended on subsistence agriculture or worked in the various government departments. The census registered only few persons working in manufacturing and transport or trade sectors.

Literacy is low in the South. Mills wrote that "more than 90 percent of the population have never attended school".[3] This low level of education is reflected in the lack of trained and skilled manpower. Efforts to re-open schools and expand enrolment were started soon after the Addis Ababa Agreement (1972). At the time of the 1973 census, there were only 145,000 students attending schools at all levels. "In a regional establishment of approaching 60,000 persons in 1975/76, 20 percent of the budget for posts remained unfilled at the end of the year. By mid-1976/77 it was estimated that approximately one-third of the establishment was unfilled."[4] The ambitious Six-Year Plan for the South (1977/78–1982/83) undoubtedly required more personnel to fill administrative, professional and technical posts.

Schools have continuously been beset by shortages of books, laboratory facilities and teachers. Very often lack of food has resulted in schools being closed down. Despite the expansion in University education in the country in general, and the opening of a University in Juba in 1977, the problem of lack of skilled manpower persists. According to Garvey-Williams and Mills (1976)[5], less than 350 students with adequate university entry qualifications emerged annually from the senior secondary schools. Even by the end of the Six-Year Plan, this figure was not expected to exceed 800 and so the problem of lack of trained, skilled manpower will persist, thus impeding development efforts. Of course, with the present war still raging, these efforts have come to a virtual standstill.

The Southern Sudan Prior to 1898

The Turco-Egyptian invasion of the Sudan in 1820/21 marked the beginning of knowledge of the land and the people of Southern Sudan so far as the outside world was concerned. The South was relatively isolated, due to the Sudd and vast swamps which were natural barriers, rendering attempts at linking Northern political units such as the

Kingdom of Kush (750–300 BC) to the Nilotes of the Upper Nile highly improbable, despite the suggestion to the contrary made by Beshir.[6]

The Turco-Egyptian invaders opened up the land to a limited extent and, as a consequence, made possible the development of the trade in ivory and later slaves. In 1839, having subdued the Nubian riverain tribes and the once-powerful Funj Kingdom, Mohamed Ali despatched a Turkish naval officer, Salim, to sail up the White Nile to discover the source of the Nile. Salim's first expedition only reached the fringes of Shilluk country; the second reached Bor in 1840 and the third reached Rejaf. This sparked off a series of explorations to discover the source of the Nile. In 1862, Speke and Grant, supported by the Royal Geographical Society in London, reached Kondokoro (near the present day Juba) where they met Samuel Baker. Another explorer, Patrick, an American, had already explored the Bahr el Ghazal in the 1850s. The discoveries of Speke, Grant and Baker settled the question of the origin and sources of the Nile, which had interested Europeans for many centuries and aroused interest in "the fertile and well-watered crescent stretching from Lake Nyansa to Lake Victoria".[7] This also prompted David Livingstone to call for "an open path for commerce and Christianity" through the Nile.[8] By 1870, a few posts in Equatoria and Bahr el Ghazal were occupied, and by 1877 the course of the White Nile between Lake Victoria and Khartoum had been completely traced.[9]

The work of explorers enabled the Turco-Egyptian authorities to establish some strongholds in the South. But the greatest significance of the opening up of the South to the outside world is that it enabled the trade in slaves to flourish. This "new route" up the White Nile became one of the busiest in the interior of Africa where European and Arab traders plundered the land for slaves and ivory. Originally it was ivory that the traders sought, often in alliance with local chiefs. However, they soon developed an interest in the prisoners captured from the local tribes and reverted to trade in them instead. Indeed, there were some Southern slave traders, such as the Zande chief Mopoi, who dealt in thousands of slaves, which he obtained either from the tribes he had conquered or from organised raids against neighbouring tribes.[10]

Under the Turco-Egyptian regime a profitable practice by European slave traders developed, based on Khartoum (founded by Mohamed Ali in 1824). They employed large numbers of armed Arab servants and founded Posts in the interior for slave trading.[11] Many of the Arab slave traders depended on capital provided by European creditors, who must be distinguished from European slave traders. The latter, together with Arab and Northern slave traders, waged a campaign of terror among Southern Sudanese tribes in their quest for slaves and ivory. The seeds of Southern Sudanese mistrust and hatred of Northerners and their

European financiers were thus implanted, with catastrophic consequences for the later history of the Sudan.

There were, however, some attempts to suppress the slave trade during this period. In 1847 Turkey denounced the slave trade and in 1860 Said, the Khedive of Egypt, prohibited slavery in his domains, including the Sudan. But the trade was too lucrative to be easily abandoned. The years 1869–1879 witnessed a struggle between Government and slave traders, the former striving to establish authority and the latter to continue their 'work'. Slave-traders, like Al Zubair Rahma and Al Aggad, were strong enough to defy Government authority and establish their own rule in certain areas. The Khedive Ismail appointed General Charles Gordon as Governor of Equatoria, with the task of stopping the slave trade amongst other things. Gordon was only partly successful in suppressing the slave trade by declaring ivory a Government monopoly and preventing the importation of arms and ammunition. Al Zubair was made Governor of Bahr el Ghazal Province in order to bring him under Government control and thereby reduce his activities as a slave merchant.[12]

Islam and Arabism hardly established themselves among the majority of Southern tribes during this period. Some tribes, like the Feroge of the Fertit group, became Muslims; but even the Islamic Elementary School built in Juba to attract Southern children to Islam had very little noticeable effect.

The Christian missionaries seem to have succeeded better than the Moslems during this period. Mohamed Ali's liberal attitude towards the missionaries encouraged them to establish themselves in the North and soon they moved southwards as well. The interests of the missionaries were to convert Negroes to Christianity and help suppress the slave trade. Two Roman Catholic Mission Stations were opened at Kondokoro and Holy Cross in 1850, and one at Kaka in 1862. But the harsh climate and prevalence of diseases hampered the work of the missionaries. Thus, the advance of Christianity, like that of Islam, was very limited in the South during this period.

The opening up of the South under the Khedive Ismail aroused European interests in the legendary riches of the South other than ivory and slaves—e.g. gold and diamonds. In any case, the European scramble for Africa and its subsequent partition was already imminent. This did not take place in the Sudan immediately, though Egypt had already been occupied by Britain in 1882. The outbreak of the Mahdi's revolt, and his triumph over the Turco-Egyptian armies in 1884, prevented it from occurring.

The Mahdist revolt against the Turco-Egyptian rule was largely, but not entirely, a Northern Sudanese matter. Holt[13] and Collins[14] have described how Southern Fertit and Nilotic tribes took part in the Mahdiya. The participation of some Southern tribes has often been used to support the claim that the Mahdist revolt was the first 'nationalist revolution' in the Sudan. But what occurred after Gordon was killed by the Mahdists in Khartoum in 1885 seems to prove otherwise.

The Mahdist control over Bahr el Ghazal was established in 1884, but the armies were soon recalled. In 1888 the second Mahdist invasion of the South began, and Captain Omer Salih established himself at Rejaf. The attempt to conquer Equatoria was resisted by the remnants of the Egyptian army, the Belgians from the neighbouring Congo and the Bari, and so the Mahdists under Arabi Dafaala were finally compelled to withdraw from Rejaf in 1897. The Belgians established their power in what came to be known as the Lado Enclave, which included all of the present Western Equatoria Province and parts of Eastern Equatoria. The Mahdist state was therefore unable to establish control over the Southern Sudan. The slave trade was greatly reduced because in the Mahdiya system "private slave trading was prohibited" by the Khalifa Abdullahi,[15] but more because the Southern tribes had a breathing space during the confusion and fighting between the Turco-Egyptian and Mahdist armies. In addition, whatever little administrative structures existed during the Turco-Egyptian period were completely destroyed. Neither the Turco-Egyptian nor the Mahdists had much more effect on the tribes in the South or in opening up of the land to the world than had the slave trade which had preceded them. In both cases, Southern resistance was considerable, albeit, disorganised.

The defeat of the Mahdists, at Rejaf in 1897 and in 1898 at Omdurman, meant that the South was once again to experience a new invader. The doors which had been opened in 1882 by the occupation of Egypt by Britain, but closed temporarily as a result of the Mahdist revolt in 1884, were re-opened. Britain invaded the Sudan in 1898 in order to achieve its grand strategy of controlling the Nile Basin. The Southern Sudan became involved in international politics and the European scramble for Africa and its partition. The direct result of the total conquest of the Sudan by the Anglo-Egyptian armies was the passing of its administration to the Condominium rulers. The scene was set for the British to play their role in determining the destiny of Southern Sudan.

The Southern Sudan and Anglo-Egyptian Rule

The reports of the early European explorers and the subsequent attempts by the Turco-Egyptian rulers to locate the source of the Nile and control it, not only encouraged the British to settle the matter of the source of the river once and for all, but also to beat other rival European powers to its control. Gray (1961)[16] provides an account of the Khedive

Ismail's attempt to outwit the British over the control of the Nile Basin. The Khedive always argued that the motives for his expansionist policies were the abolition of the slave trade, a tune Europeans wanted to hear. But the most determinant factor in the Anglo-Egyptian occupation of the Southern Sudan was to secure control of Nile Waters. In most parts of Africa, Christian missionaries were often the first to penetrate into tribal land and the solders and colonial administrators followed. In this way missionaries opened the way for European Imperialism. The story was different in Southern Sudan. "Rather than paving the way for the British occupation, the missionaries found the Southern secured by the soldiers who had preceded them. Moreover, they failed to create, in these early years, a class of accommodators prepared to cooperate with the alien administration."[17]

Unlike King Leopold of Belgium in the Congo, the British decision to occupy Southern Sudan was not influenced by the often exaggerated stories about its riches (e.g. gold, copper, ivory and rubber). The slave trade (often disguised as trade in ivory) was abhorred by the Christian Churches and European humanitarian organisations, and so 'legitimate' trade was encouraged. To do this, the river route to the south had to be explored and opened up. As this process continued the 'rumours' about vast untapped resources in Southern Sudan spread. But this 'obsession' "had virtually no influence upon the men who made the policies and decisions of the British Government".[18] To the British, the remoteness of the South from the sea and the markets of the Near East and Europe could not offset the huge costs that would be incurred in exploiting these 'potential' resources.

From the time Britain occupied Egypt and the Suez Canal in 1882, Egypt's total dependence on the Nile Waters for its very existence was readily accepted. Although at that time little was known about the hydrological features of the Nile and its tributaries and conditions at its source, the decision to occupy the Sudan and the Upper Nile was made as a matter of strategic importance. No other power should be allowed to control the Nile Basin as the Fashoda Incident of 1898 clearly showed.[19] At that time, the French, led by Captain Marchand, crossed from the west in the Congo to a small village on the bank of the White Nile called Fashoda and claimed the area for the French. Kitchener rushed from Khartoum to Fashoda and met Marchand in full military readiness for armed confrontation. However, the two men decided to refer the dispute to London and Paris for a diplomatic solution rather than fight it out in the battle-field. Under the threat of war France capitulated, recalled Marchand, and sought reconciliation with England. This incident at Fashoda (later renamed Kodok to save the French a perpetual stigma on their national pride) was the turning point for the future of the Southern Sudan. If it had become a French colony, certainly its modern history would have been totally different, for better or worse. The important point is that the incident made the British more determined than ever to speed up the total conquest of the whole Upper Nile and establish a firm grip over it. Thus, using its technological and military power, as well as diplomacy, Britain laboured to secure all the Nile Basin and keep out the Belgians and the French. As an imperial power it had no choice but to rule, despite the lack of definitive information and knowledge about the hydrology of the Nile and the potentials of the land within its basin.

The Southern Sudan was also of strategic importance to the British in that, with its conquest, the dream of constructing a railway from Cape Town in South Africa to Cairo could then become realisable. The Southern Sudan was the missing link. The idea never came to fruition but it was a factor in the decision to occupy the Southern Sudan.

The technical and organisational superiority of the British forces made possible the conquest, occupation and administration of the Southern Sudan. Perhaps this was best demonstrated by the clearance of the Sudd, thereby opening up the interior to British forces, who could then be transported by steamers up the Nile to Bahr el-Ghazal and Equatoria. There was very little the tribes of the Southern Sudan could do to stop the occupation of their land.

However, there was a considerable amount of resistance to this invasion, just as there had been resistance to previous occupations. The resistance of the people of Southern Sudan to the British invasion was sporadic, disorganised and certainly uncoordinated. The Shilluk offered a more co-ordinated resistance under their King (Reth) but their greater numbers could not match the fire-power of the British Maxim guns. The Latuka, in Eastern Equatoria, offered ferocious resistance but by 1912 they were subdued, since the British "were using light mountain artillery against them with devastating effect".[20] In Western Equatoria, the Azande, under chiefs Yambio, Basungada, Gangura and a score of others, also fought against the British at first. But later Yambio decided to co-operate with the British and Basungada and Gangura were exiled. Collaboration was rewarded with British assurance of continued rule and support against enemy tribes. The Azande Chief Tombura and the Dinka prophet Ariendit are instances of Southern chiefs who acknowledged British rule because it served their interests to do so, mainly in return for British support in their fight against neighbouring hostile tribes.

There were rebellions against the British, like that of the Agar Dinka in 1902, the Atout Dinka in 1910, and the Aliab Dinka in 1919 but it is beyond the scope and purpose of this book to analyse the various instances of Southern resistance. Suffice it to say that up to 1923, the British could not bring large parts of the South under their effective rule. Up to that date, the Annuak, Toposa and Turkana (along the portion of the Sudan-Ethiopian border that is in the South-East of the Region) were left alone. In addition, pockets of Nuer both east and west of Bahr el Zeraf and also of Dinka south of Bahr el Arab, remained outside British control also.

For the past hundred years the history of the Southern Sudan can be seen as a continuing process of resistance to the various alien invaders, beginning with their appearance in the middle of the nineteenth century. The second feature of this resistance is that, both during the slave trade period and at the time of the British invasion, some tribal leaders (e.g. Tombura and Ariendit) not only gave up the fight but also collaborated with the intruders. Thirdly, the organisation of resistance was dependent upon the internal organisation of the tribal groups or sections themselves and their relationships with their neighbours. "Thus, in the highly centralised Azande chiefdoms resistance was organised by the Avungura chiefs who led their well-disciplined military companies against the invaders".[21] But among the Nilotes (e.g. Dinka), "the organisation of resistance developed forms which were the direct reflection of the character of the Nilotic societies".[22] Every man was a warrior who defended his cattle camp against outsiders. Fighting a force such as the British required a level of co-ordination and military discipline that only a centralised command could muster. The Nilotic political system had no such centralised command. "Instead, traditional and perhaps even reactionary tribal divisions continued to weaken the Nilotic resistance to British rule."[23]

The impact of Southern Sudanese resistance was felt more by the colonial administration in the Sudan and Egypt than by the Foreign Office, since the British Governor-General was expected to deal with such matters with little policy interference from London. "In matters of the Upper Nile, the British in Cairo were concerned *only* about the Nile waters ..."[24] Local administrative, political and military matters were left in the hands of the Governor-General. Some Governor-Generals, like Wingate in 1916, were hardly enthusiastic about the South. The need to "pacify" the South was hampered by a shortage of finance for military and administrative purposes so many parts remained outside the sphere of influence of the British. Where "Pax Britannica" existed the colonial administrators were able to collect taxes and establish some economic and social infrastructures. The crucial points, however, are that the destiny of the people of Southern Sudan was determined by an alien power and for the first time in its history the South was identified as an integral part of the Sudan.

Thus, motivated mainly by the desire to control the whole Nile Basin and the Nile waters, the British annexed Southern Sudan and laboured to keep out other European competitors. However, though the commercial and Christian missionary motives for the conquest were less significant in precipitating the conquest, these factors gained more prominence once 'pacification' and a colonial administrative structure were established.

The first task of the British, apart from establishing communications between north and south, was the imposition of the Pax Britannica upon a land that had not known peace for the best part of twenty to thirty years. The watchword of the British was 'indirect rule' in the South as it was in many other parts of British colonial Africa.[25] Recognising the racial, cultural and religious differences between the northern and southern parts of the Sudan, the British endeavoured to protect the traditional way of life of the southern people from the influence of the predominantly Arab, Moslem North. This policy continued with the establishment of the 1930 'Southern Policy'. Mac Michael officially stated: "The policy of the Government in the Southern Sudan is to build up a series of self-contained racial and tribal units with structure and organisation based, to whatever extent the requirements of equity and good government permit, upon indigenous customs, traditional usage and beliefs."[26]

Probably an important reason for the formation of such a policy was that, if the South was to be governed effectively, the confidence of the people in their masters must be gained. This confidence could not be won if the fear of Southerners of a return to the Mahdiya was fostered by the presence of too many Arab traders. Although these Arabs were not slave traders, Southerners still remembered the sufferings they sustained at that time. They actually remembered the slave trade and not just because missionaries reminded them of it in schools, as is often vigorously claimed by Northern Sudanese writers.[27] The effect slavery has on people is such that it does not need anyone, missionary or otherwise, to constantly remind them of it. The argument that Christian missionaries encouraged the memories of slave trade in the minds of Southerners is at best political propaganda. Slavery affected generations of Southern tribesmen long before the missionaries came to their land. Memories of slavery were recounted to generations of Southern children by their elders over the years. Even the few children who attended missionary schools did not need to be reminded of what was vividly already imprinted in their minds by their parents. Probably the main reason for the introduction of the Southern Policy, however, was that it was dictated by the thorough-going implementation of indirect rule.

In practice, the Southern Policy meant that Northern administrative and military presence was kept at negligible levels. Northern traders were restricted and had to obtain permits. The use of Arabic and Arab dress (like the one called *Jellabia)* were prohibited, or at least discouraged. This policy progressed sufficiently for the British to begin to think, after the end of the war in 1945, of 'separating' the South from the North and annexing at least parts of it to British East Africa. However in 1946 Arab Nationalism in the Middle East was reaching new heights, so the most 'sensible' choice open to the British seemed to be a cautious granting of independence to the Sudan, while retaining their bases at the Suez Canal. Northern politicians increased their demand for the abolition of the Southern Policy and the total annexation of the South to the North. Thus, the Southern Policy was abandoned in 1946 and an All Sudan Legislative Assembly was opened in 1948. The process leading to independence in 1956 had thus been set in motion. Southern fears and worries about possible replacement of the British masters by Northern Sudanese were temporarily allayed by the promise of a federal status within a United Sudan. But, alas, that autonomous status was to come only after seventeen years of civil war in which all developments in the south came to a halt and many lives were lost, with many people deserting their lands and property and fleeing to neighbouring countries.[28] An account of the horrors and atrocities of that war is not the concern of this book. The important question is what went Wrong?

Far too often the North, through its politicians and scholars,[29] blamed the causes of the Southern Rebellion of 1955/56 and the subsequent war that ensued, on the *divide et impere* policies of the British. The British prevented the spread of Islam, and Arabic in the South while encouraging Christianity and English. Christian missionaries reminded Southerners of the slave trade. The South, they argued, is landlocked and economically enviable on its own and thus must depend on the North.

The Southern Sudan has always resisted foreign invaders, including the British. Thus, from the southern viewpoint, the British Southern Policy of 1930 was indeed based on realism and pragmatism. It is ironic that the 1972 Addis Ababa Agreement[30] implemented what the British had basically been pursuing all along; that all Northern administrators be replaced by Southerners. The Agreement stated that the entire civil service in the Southern Regions should be run by Southerners under an autonomous Regional Governments in Juba, Wau and Malakal. Northern traders could only operate by obtaining a trading licence from the Southern Regional Ministries of Commerce. The police and prisons forces were to be manned by Southerners. Even the composition of the army in the South was to be a mixture of Northerners and Southerners. Local Government, education, internal trade and communications and regional planning were all to be matters that concerned the regions. Only matters related to foreign policy, national planning defence and foreign trade were left in the hands of the Khartoum Government.

The British must bear a good deal of responsibility for the events that were triggered off by the 1955 mutiny of the Equatoria Corps at Torit. After succumbing to Northern Sudanese and Egyptian pressure to abandon the Southern Policy, the British reversed their policy completely. British commercial interests in the North would have been jeopardised if they had followed a "separate" policy towards the South again. The Gezira Scheme (started in 1925) provided Lancashire with cotton, and the Mahdist UMMA Party was a close British ally. The British wanted to leave behind an ally that would foster their interests in the post-independence Sudan. The National Unionist Party (NUP), the political wing of the Khatmiya religious Islamic sect, supported Sudan's unity with Egypt, a prospect the British could not contemplate. Thus, they abandoned their earlier policy of protecting the traditional way of life of the peoples living in the south from the influence of the predominantly Arab, Moslem north in 1953 when, in principle, the British decided to grant the Sudan independence. The previous separatist policies, meant that only three Southerners were available to fill top civil service posts, out of a total of nine hundred for all the country, when 'Sudanization' was then introduced. This great discrepancy, in part, led to the Torit Mutiny which was put down by the British Governor-General, using Northern troops. The details of this Southern rebellion are available elsewhere,[31] however, the participation of the British in ending it shows that they had abandoned their earlier policies. Commercial interests and pragmatism prevailed over their best moral judgement.

Origins of the Present War

It is not our intention, nor is it possible here, to provide a comprehensive account of the reasons that led to the current war that has been raging in Southern Sudan since 1985 or even a bit earlier on. We therefore provide only a cursory glance at the main factors that sparked a new war after the 13 years of relative peace and security that followed the implementation of the Addis Ababa Accord in 1972. It was a period of only relative peace because some Anyanya forces never accepted the Addis Agreement which they regarded as a sell out to the North. Certainly Southern Sudanese leaders like Gordon Mourtat (still in self-imposed exile in London) or the late Aggrey Jaden never subscribed to the Addis Accord.

Various incidents during the course of the 13 years of relative peace showed that some Southerners were still in arms in the bush; for example the Akobo Incident, the Wau Rebellion by an Anyanya Captain, and the 1976 Juba Airport Mutiny. Long before Colonel John Garang fled into the bush following the Army's bombardment of rebellious troops in Bor under the command of Captain Kerbino, Anyanya 11 was already active in the bush, especially in Upper Nile. In fact, in his attempt to usurp the leadership of all the fighting forces in the bush, Garang had to wage a fierce war against Anyanya II under the leadership of Akot Atem and Gai Tut whom he killed in the process. This has created an enmity between Anyanya II (largely dominated by Nuer) and SPLA (Dinka Bor dominated). Untold numbers of Southerners have died because of this rivalry.

John Garang, a Southern Sudanese officer in the Sudan armed forces, lead the second rebellion in 1983, which attracted most of the major political forces in the south. Sudan People's Liberation Army and its political wing Sudan People's Liberation Movement (and not South Sudan Liberation Movement) were duly established. By 1985 John Garang's SPLA was dominant in the bush but it was still based in Ethiopia where it was enjoying the facilities of the former Radio Voice of the Gospel for its own clandestine SPLA Radio to tell the world of the intention or aims of the SPLM.

Samuel Makinda sums up the causes of the war as follows:

> "These issues—the introduction of Islamic law, the subdivision of the South, and the deprivation of oil revenues—convinced some Southerners to take up arms to regain autonomy. They became guerrillas, first of ANYANYA II which seeks secession, and later of the Sudan People's Liberation Army, which aims to unite Sudan under a socialist government run by Southerners."[32]

Certainly, it is widely understood and generally accepted that most (if not all) Southerners condemn the introduction of the *Sharia Laws* by General Numeri in September 1983 (i.e. a few months after the escape of John Garang into the bush). Almost immediately, the three Regional Assemblies in Wau Juba and Malakal passed resolutions condemning the Sharia or September Laws as they are sometimes called. Huge demonstrations followed in the three main towns of the South calling for their repeal or removal. Instead of heeding this President Numeri proceeded to implement these laws, and many innocent Southerners lost their limbs and some were hanged for such crimes as theft, drinking or selling alcohol, fornication or adultery, etc. The largely Christian/animist South still refuses to accept *Sharia Laws* and they demand a return to secular laws as existed in the 1956 constitution amended in 1964. It could be said therefore, that the continued existence of *Sharia Laws* in the Sudan, fuels the current war.

The redivision of the South is a more contentious reason for the war. It is true that it was mainly the people of Equatoria who called for it in 1981 as an internal administrative arrangement to diffuse possible tribal conflicts (e.g. Bari-Dinka Bor conflicts over grazing land and agricultural land use); to devolve political and administrative power in a manner that ensured a wider local participation rather than concentration in Juba; and since the North had been further re-divided from one to six regions, the south should also be similarly divided so as to enjoy equal privileges and rights. This "Equatoria" view was not accepted by some Southerners who argued that re-division weakened the position of the South vis-à-vis the North and that it was based on a "groundless" fear of Dinka domination. In all, these controversial views persist and it is reasonable to assume that some Southerners might have taken to the bush because of re-division, especially those who had lost positions of power, wealth and influence because of it.

The manifesto of the SPLM/SPLA[33] does not mention the above points explicitly although their broadcasts do. According to the SPLM/SPLA the war is not for secession of the South from the North, but one for achieving social justice and equality in the Sudan. It is a war to overhaul the present oppressive system led by an (undefined) minority in Khartoum and replace it with a socialist system whereby power will be shared equally by all and, above all, national wealth will be fairly distributed. These 'nationalist' goals continue to dominate SPLM/SPLA propaganda but leave a lot of questions unanswered. What is the SPLM/SPLA agenda for the South? Is there an agenda (hidden) for the South? It is not uncommon to find many Southerners asking these questions because they have a direct bearing on why they are suffering this war and what can they hope for in the future.

The 17-years war stemmed from clear causes well known to all Southerners and Northerners, i.e. race and religious differences, cultural differences and political and economic imbalances. The political attitude of Southerners at that time, can be summed up by the following quotation attributed to Joseph Oduho from Anthony Carthew's article in the Daily Mail (London) in 1966:

> "Our political attitude has hardened from one where we would have accepted some kind of loose federation with the North to a demand for secession, complete independence for the South."

It is worth mentioning that the single most important condition Southerners demanded before accepting independence for a united Sudan was their being granted federal status within it. Oduho is referring to the hardening of the position of Southerners from federation to separation between 1956 and the end of the 17-year war in 1972. Again some questions could be asked with regard to the present war. Is its agenda the same as that of the 17-year war? Could it be that the SPLA itself is multi-faceted in that some adhere to the principles of Anyanya I (1955–72) and others to those in its declared manifesto?

We pose the above questions for the purpose of understanding the complexities of the present war, but suffice it to say here that war still rages with devastating effects on human and physical resources and is directly affecting the economy adversely.

Chapter 2

Pre-Independence State of the Economy

Agriculture

Agriculture was and still is by far the main source of livelihood of the vast majority of the people. In Upper Nile Province, the most extensively cultivated crops were dura and maize; other crops of lesser and limited cultivation included simsim, groundnuts, cotton, beans and tobacco. Shifting cultivation with long fallow was widely used.[34]

The best available study of agriculture in the Sudan during the pre-independence period, is Tothill's book in which he describes agriculture in the old Upper Nile and Equatoria provinces.[35] Tothill wrote of the Upper Nile: "Generally speaking, the cattle-owning Nilotic is an improvident and poor cultivator, growing only barely enough grain, with the minimum amount of work, to maintain him and his small family until the following season. When crops fail, the hunger situation becomes acute and often necessitates the undertaking of famine relief by Government and the importation of grain from the north".[36]

It would seem, therefore, that Tothill explained the low level of agricultural production in the province by blaming the Nilotics for emphasising animal husbandry more than cultivation. For example, cotton was introduced to Upper Nile in 1923 to enable people to obtain cash for paying taxes and to purchase cloth, soap, salt, etc. The response of the Nilotes to the new crop was so poor that the highest amount ever produced before independence was 760 tons of raw cotton.[37] Attempts were made to produce sesame as a cash crop, as well as for local consumption. Local consumption demand for sesame oil was fairly high. But again Tothill argued that despite this demand, local farmers were unwilling to adopt new crops like sesame, sweet potatoes or cassava.[38]

Unfortunately, Tothill does not let us know why, apart from his emphasis on livestock raising, the Nilotic farmer was apparently indifferent towards efforts by the colonial administration to distribute free seeds of cotton, groundnuts, sesame, etc. If the Nilotes cared more for their livestock and less for crop cultivation, then they must have had good reason to do so. Further, the condition of the soils in Upper Nile are unsuitable for certain crops (e.g. groundnuts are difficult to harvest because the soil is too sticky). Since only hand-hoes were used, increased production in terms of area and intensity of cultivation could not be expected. Furthermore, the crops which the colonial administration introduced were either cash crops, like cotton or of little local importance, e.g. sweet potatoes, cassava, groundnuts, etc. Dura (sorghum) was, and still is, the main staple and is consumed with meat and dairy products.

The state of agriculture in the old Equatoria Province was broadly similar to that in the Upper Nile. But whereas agriculture in the Upper Nile supplemented animal production, it was often the main and only source of livelihood in Equatoria. In Equatoria, unlike in the Upper Nile, mixed cropping was widely practised. The main combinations have been listed by Tothill as follows: "sesame and elusine; sesame, elusine and sorghum; maize and cowpeas; and maize and pumpkin".[39] This was a good method of sowing. In most cases seed was scattered over the field by hand, except maize, groundnut and sometimes cowpea and some types of sorghum which were planted in small holes. Okra, Jew's mallows, gourds and tobacco were also grown together with certain types of fruit trees and vegetables.

One of the commonest problems in both Upper Nile and Equatoria was the damage caused to crops by pests and diseases. Tothill noted that most parts of Equatoria had the added problem of soil erosion.[40] This was mainly sheet erosion, particularly in the iron-stone plateau. An important factor that contributed to general erosion is that people set fire to grass every year when hunting or collecting honey, in some parts over-grazing led to more erosion. But, despite this, the use of animal dung by those who owned cattle lessened the problem.

Agriculture was for subsistence. The methods employed and the tools used (e.g. hand-hoes) were "primitive". Nevertheless, as was stated by the Southern Development Team, "these methods were developed over centuries of trial and error and therefore exposed the cultivator to minimum production risks caused by the erratic environment but on the whole satisfied the simple needs of simple people."[41]

Animal Husbandry

The people of the Upper Nile province are mainly cattle herders in varying degrees of specialisation; the Dinka, for example, being more so than the Shilluk, but agriculture has always been supplementary to animal husbandry. The trade-off between crop production and cattle rearing has always held the balance between famine and subsistence.

The following table shows the best available data on livestock in the South prior to independence.

Table 1. *Livestock Numbers in the Southern Provinces According to Environmental Regions (1954)*

Region	Cattle	Sheep and goats
Central Rain lands	60,500	80,000
Flood	1,561,500	1,444,000
Equatorial	775,000	2,562,000

Source: Southern Development Team (1955), ibid., p. 107.

Clearly, Upper Nile (which lies within the flood region) has a higher number of livestock than either Equatoria or Bahr el Ghazal Provinces. A number of factors have helped to keep this sizeable population of animals in check; the most important were, and still are, the ravages of rinderpest and pleuro-pneumonia. Trypanosomiasis and foot and mouth disease also added to the death toll.

Grazing patterns follow an annual seasonal migratory cycle. After the cessation of the rains, when the grass is drying off, the Nilotic herdsman moves his stock down to the river where grazing is rich, and remains there throughout the dry season until the beginning of the next rainy season. Cattle are also grazed, as for example by the Shilluk, on large islands in the rivers during the dry season. Tothill wrote about the quality of the Nilotic cattle that "on the whole the cattle are rich milkers, having a butter fat content over 4 percent, but poor quality producers, 5 pints a day usually. An average Nilotic steer will kill out at about 6 cwt. of good beef, dead weight".[42]

Despite the emphasis so often laid on the reluctance of nomads and even semi-nomadic pastoralists, such as the Dinka and Nuer, to sell stock, large quantities of cattle on the hoof were, in fact, exported North. Table 2 shows exports of hides between 1949 and 1951. In the absence of actual figures of sales of livestock and exports to other parts of the country, these figures along with those in Table 3, provide the only practical way of estimating cattle sales. The total number of hides exported was certainly small compared to the overall potential in the South as seen in Table 1 above, but the trend showed an increase in the volume of cattle exports to the North.

Some internal trade in cattle took place within the South as well. Table 3, taken from the same source as Table 2, shows the number of cattle on the hoof sold to the "fly-belt" of Equatoria Province from Bahr el Ghazal Province.

Table 2. *Exports of Cattle Hides from Bahr el Ghazal and the Upper Nile Provinces to the North (1949 to 1951)*

Province	Town or village of export	No. of hides 1949	No. of hides 1950	No. of hides 1951
Bahr el Ghazal	Wau	39,820	22,117	28,480
	Shambe	177	7,437	4,185
	Rumbek	14,945	12,668	6,730
	Tonj	6,711	2,142	381
	Gogrial	5,748	5,560	6,353
	Aweil	748	5,876	6,424
TOTAL		68,149	55,800	52,553
Upper Nile	Bentiu	3,515	4,220	Nil
	Adok	11,664	11,048	15,773
	Wankai	12,417	7,203	39,304
	Bor	10,830	17,449	14,682
	Nasir	11,453	19,321	13,866
	Malakal	10,961	11,575	4,825
TOTAL		60,842	70,816	88,450

Source: Jack, J. D. M., "Food Resources of Animal Origin in the Sudan", paper presented at the 1953 conference of the Philosophical Society of the Sudan on Food and Society in Sudan (p. 18).

The figures in Table 3, show a marked increase in the trade over the period. If figures for cattle from Upper Nile Province could be added to these, we would then be able to appreciate the volume and importance of this trade. It is worth noting that the figures show "institutional" demand of towns, government stations, schools, and missions. No account was taken of the demand of the general population, such as the Zande and other tribes who inhabit the "fly-belt". The vast majority of the people of the "fly-belt" relied on game, particularly wild pigs, for their meat.

Table 3. *Cattle on the Hoof from Bahr el Ghazal Province to the "Fly-Belt" of Equatoria Province (1949–1953)*

Year	No. of cattle	Approx. weight in kilos of fresh meat less bone*	Approx. weight in tons of fresh meat less bone
May 1949 to 31/12/1949	684	71,820	72
1/1/1950 to 30/6/1951	2,002	210,210	210
1/7/1951 to 30/6/1952	2,548	267,540	2,647
1/7/1952 to 30/6/1953	2,968	311,640	311
TOTAL	8,202	861,210	3,240

*Figures calculated on the assumption that the average live weight of a bull was 300 kilos and dressed weight 150 kilos, of which 30 percent would be bone.

Colonial Economic Policy Towards the South

Before I go on to discuss the Zande Scheme as an aspect of colonial "development policy", a brief explanation of the nature and reasons why the South lagged behind the North seems useful.

After "pacifying" and establishing law and order in the whole country, the Condominium rulers began to pursue a policy of "separate" but unequal development of the North and the South. The proximity of the North to the sensitive Middle East Zone and its strategic importance to both Egypt and Britain are among some of the reasons why the North became an area for active British investment. A network of rail links were built, dams were constructed and the Gezira Scheme came to life. No comparable development activity was taking place in the South. Whereas the introduction of cotton into the South was only on a small scale, cotton production in the Gezira was performed through the establishment of a large-scale modern irrigation scheme. It is often argued that the North had a comparative advantage for the production of such crops as cotton, due to its higher level of labour productivity and relative abundance of economic and social infrastructures, which are essential prerequisites for modern investment undertakings.[43] Beshir has argued that because the country's only port lies in the North, it was justifiable to first concentrate development efforts in the North before moving to the South. Another view often propounded is that British colonial interests lay with the North which could provide raw cotton and gum Arabic, commodities which the South could not provide on a competitive basis.

The relative neglect of the South was clearly manifest from the "Southern Policy" of the forties as well as the colonial indecision about the future of the South—e.g. uniting it with the North; annexing it to East Africa; or granting it independence. It was only when a united Sudan seemed imminent that ideas for the development of the South began to appear and partly led to the formation of the Southern Development Team (1954) which was entrusted with the task of determining the natural resources and development potential of the Southern Sudan. The most important conclusion it reached was that the South could at least produce supplementary goods which could not be produced in the North for climatic reasons, and which were then imported from abroad. Table 4 lists principal imports into the Sudan of commodities which could be produced in the South because the environmental conditions were favourable for such production. Cotton is not included because it was already being produced in the North.

Both the climate and soils in Eastern Equatoria and parts of Western Equatoria are good for the production of tea, coffee and tobacco. Sugar cane could be produced along the Bahr el Gebel and, indeed, the Mongalla Sugar Complex was established for that purpose. Rice could be grown in the marshy lands in Aweil district in Bahr el Ghazal Province. In general, all the crops listed in Table 4 were introduced and produced in the South with some success.

Table 4. *Principal Imports into the Sudan of Commodities which could be produced in the South**

Commodity	Quantity (tons)	Value ('000)		% total imports value	
	1953	1953	1954	1953	1954
Sugar	89,710	3,833	3,654	7.6	7.5
Tea	4,932	1,240	3,545	2.5	7.3
Coffee	6,125	2,160	1,878	4.3	3.9
Tobacco & Cigarettes	559	881	749	1.7	1.5
Rice	1,400	123	158	0.2	0.3
TOTAL	–	8,239	9,984	16.3	20.5

*Source: Sudan Almanac, 1955, taken from Basinski, in *Sudan Notes and Records*, 1956–58 (p. 26).

The Zande Scheme

The Zande Scheme best illustrates the efforts made by the colonial administration to introduce some comprehensive development programmes in the South. The projects purported aim was to improve the living conditions of at least some of the people of the South. It was a public sector enterprise, whereas the coffee, tea and tobacco schemes were owned by private Greek, Syrian, Lebanese and Northern Sudanese businessmen. Tothill, the then Director of Agriculture in the Sudan (1944) and proponent of the Zande Scheme, called it 'An Experiment in the Social Emergence of a Remote Area'. The scheme aimed at "nothing less than the complete social emergence and the social and economic stability of the Zande people".[44]

Briefly, the Zande Scheme aimed to establish some agroindustries; improve education and provide more health and social services. The scheme was to provide for the growing of cotton, ginning it, spinning the lint and weaving it at a mill to be established at Anzara. The cloth was to be sold within the Sudan to reduce import of cloth which was 1,500 tons annually at that time.[45] Cotton growing was to be introduced as an integral part of an improved native agricultural system designed so that each household produced on its own farm adequate food and sufficient cotton to bring in a serviceable income. Cotton manufacturing was supposed to provide increased income to the producer. Provision was made for the production of soap from cotton seed and locally produced palm oil; for the growing and curing of Robusta coffee; and for the growing of sugar cane. These provisions were made in such a way as to involve the household unit as central to the agricultural production process as well as in consumption of the manufactured products.

Another project designed to utilise local products was the establishment of a saw-mill to produce timber to replace imported building material. Commodities which could not be produced from the area, like meat, would be imported from other parts of the South.

An essential part of the scheme was the provision of controlled shops throughout the experimental area to deal with local raw and manufactured products and to supply imports at the lowest possible prices. A board was to run the different production and distribution sections of the scheme.

Tothill chose the Zande area for his experiment because, in his words, "it was so remote from overseas markets that there was no prospect of achieving social emergence on the basis of exports to places beyond the Sudan; and the good agricultural climate, some good soil and a reasonably dense population ensured that the raw materials required could be produced satisfactorily.[46] The scheme, if successful, would become a model for development in the South as well as the rest of the Sudan. It is not our intention to evaluate the success or failure of the Zande Scheme, but merely to cite it as the only major development effort of any note embarked upon during this Pre-Independence Period. However, as Reining[47] and Barnett[48] have argued, the undertaking failed to meet the aspirations of the Zande and has not developed sufficiently to become a model for development in the South and the rest of the Sudan. This is not to say that the scheme was a total failure, particularly when we consider the fact that almost as soon as it started operation, the civil war in the south broke out. It was only after the Accord in 1972 that the Zande Scheme was revived. Most other projects had either been destroyed or neglected during the civil war (1955–72). Government presence and activity during that period was largely military and destructive. Thus, the March 1972 Peace Accord in Addis Ababa was a landmark in the development of the South because once again 'development' could be promoted.

Chapter 3

The Post Independence State of the Economy (1956–1983)

Agriculture

Subsistence agriculture and traditional animal husbandry are still by far the most important economic activities. The rich potential for agricultural development in the South was described by the Southern Development Investigation Team (1955).[49] Most of that report, as well as the chapters on agriculture in Tothill's book (1948) would apply today: these are the possibilities of growing food crops (e.g. sorghum, millet, groundnuts, maize, beans, cassava, rice, vegetables and fruit) and the potential for cash crops (e.g. cotton, sugarcane, tobacco, tea and coffee), as well as exploitation of the livestock, fish and forest resources and more recently oil in Bentiu area.

Levels of agricultural production are difficult to estimate. "There has never been an agricultural census in the South nor has any systematic collection of statistics been undertaken."[50] Table 5 shows crop production in the Region during the 1960s. The Six-Year Plan for the Southern Region (1977/78–1982/83) contains more recent data.

The food crops in Table 5 do not include cassava and other root crops which are staple foods in some parts. In 1971/72 some 8,000 feddans were planted with rice grown under flood cultivation in Aweil district. Also excluded are coffee plantations (about 2,000 feddans), tea (2,000 feddans) and oil palms (300 feddans).[51] Generally, crop yields are not significantly different from the national average.

Let us now discuss the then existing and future (planned) prospects for crop production taking each crop separately. Sorghum was produced all over the Region and constituted the staple food grain. The Six-Year Plan purported to increase acreage from 875,000 feddans (1976) to 1,326,000 feddans by 1982/83. To achieve this target, the Regional Government created a programme of agricultural extension to promote better cultural practices; a programme of seed distribution (undertaken by the Project Development Unit of the Regional Ministry of Agriculture); and the introduction of ox-ploughing. The success of the programme of agricultural extension was hampered by the inability of extension workers to reach farmers due to lack of transport or lack of fuel. The establishment of communications links between farmers, extension workers and the head office in Juba took longer than the plan period. In many cases farmers consumed the seed distributed because they were hungry.

Table 5. *Crop Production in Southern Sudan, 1960/61 to 1968/69 ('000 Feddans) (Annual Figures)*

	Cotton	Sorghum	Millet*	Maize	Sesame	Ground nuts	Horse beans	All gross
1960/61	33.5	323.2	84.6	67.8	37.6	96.3	1.4	664.4
1961/62	36.9	316.0	45.8	27.5	31.7	95.4	1.5	554.8
1962/63	35.2	382.1	55.5	55.4	39.3	104.3	5.0	676.8
1963/64	29.3	332.1	52.2	43.7	36.0	102.0	1.7	596.9
1964/65	2.0	301.8	22.2	27.0	31.6	64.7	–	449.3
1965/66	–	245.5	14.3	12.9	29.8	46.6	–	349.1
1966/67	–	297.8	6.9	12.3	11.5	16.9	–	345.3
1967/68	–	244.0	8.5	16.2	8.5	30.6	–	307.8
1968/69	2.3	313.7	7.8	20.5	178.1+	53.5	–	575.8

* Millet (Dukhn) plus Finger Millet (Ellusine).
+ A satisfactory explanation for the vast expansion in 1968/69 is not available.

Source: Bulletin of Agricultural Statistics of the Sudan 1968/69.

In some parts of Western Equatoria Province cassava constituted the main diet. The area under cultivation was roughly 110,000 feddans. By 1982/83 it was planned that this would be increased to 167,000 feddans. Cassava was becoming a substitute for sorghum (particularly in areas where sorghum was often in short supply like the towns) and this had acted as an incentive for farmers to grow more. Maize production was being encouraged by the government. The strategy for this involved distribution of improved seed varieties, provision of grinding mills, marketing facilities and the introduction of the ox-plough. The response of farmers to the introduction of new quick maturing varieties of maize had generally been favourable, largely because a quick maize harvest averted hunger. Furthermore, the possibility of earning cash income from the sale of the crop in towns encouraged farmers, but a comparable response had not taken place. A similar strategy was being followed for groundnut production. Ox-ploughing was experimented with in parts of Lakes Province but it had not yet attracted farmers.

Rice had great potentialities both as a large scale cash crop and as a supplementary crop for small farmers. A scheme for the production of upland rice was already in operation in Aweil, financed through a multi-lateral aid programme and the Regional Development Budget. The claim by the officials of the Regional Ministry of Agriculture that the scheme was a success was supported by the availability of Aweil rice in the shops in Juba, Wau and other major towns. However, small farmers had not started to grow the crop.

In 1976, the total cotton production was about 10,000 tons from an area of some 33,000 feddans.[52] The Six-Year Plan aimed to increase cotton production to 25,000 tons by 1982/83. The amount of cotton produced was inadequate to meet the requirements of Nzara and Mongalla Spinning and Weaving factories and the deficit was met by imports from the North.

The Government aimed to make the Sudan self-sufficient in coffee. Several varieties could be grown. Along a narrow strip of land parallel to the Zaire border, the land is suitable for growing Robusta coffee. Small areas in the Imatong mountains and on Boma plateau are suitable for Arabica coffee, while in parts of Yei District, Excelea coffee showed promising results. The government's development strategy called for the distribution of seeds and seedlings to small-holders and assisting them with credit facilities and guaranteed minimum purchasing prices. While emphasis was on small-holder promotion, the government hoped to run several large estates—some already in production and others requiring rehabilitation. Private investors were also encouraged to establish large plantations and processing facilities. The area under coffee then was about 3,000 feddans.[53] By the end of the plan the area was expected to have increased to 15,000 feddans; 11,000 feddans under small-holder production, 2,000 feddans of Government estates and 2,000 feddans under private management. It is difficult to say whether these targets could have been reached. However, the fact that the demand for coffee was undoubtedly high, particularly in the North (coffee beans were often transported by plane), might have encouraged farmers.

Tea holds considerable promise for development. The Sudan was importing well over 20,000 tons of tea per year. By 1983 it was expected that demand would be approaching 26,000 tons. In both East and West Equatoria, it is possible to grow tea at heights over 3,000 feet. In 1974 an FAO feasibility study recommended the establishment of 12 tea plantations, each of 500 feddans, near Iwatoka, Yei, Katire and Gilo. By 1983 some 200 feddans had been established and it was the government's intention to extend this area to 6,000 feddans by the end of the Six-Year Plan. The government envisaged factory facilities and a range of employment opportunities from nursery and plantation work to tea packing and marketing. As for coffee, increased tea production seemed possible. However, processing it locally was not realised.

An analysis of the agricultural sector would not be complete without a look at the forestry sector. Almost half of the Southern Region is covered by forest vegetation of varying types, ranging from savannah woodlands and swamps in the north and centre, to the gallery forest on the mountains in the south. As a whole the Region accounts for over 90 percent of the national forest resources. The requirement for timber in the Sudan in 1983 was approximately 60,000 cubic metres a year. In 1966 the figure had been less than 6,000 cubic metres.[54] By 1982/83 it was estimated that national demand would rise to 90,000 cubic metres per annum, and again the Government hoped that the Southern Region would satisfy it.

Most of the inland fisheries resources are concentrated in the Southern Region. Estimates of potential production for the whole country were put at up to 165,000 tons per annum.[55] Up to 155,000 tons of these were accounted for by the Southern Region. By the end of the Six-Year Plan it was hoped that the production of fish would have increased from less than 5,000 tons per annum to 21,000 tons. To achieve this goal various sectorial programmes were envisaged. Although the Department of Fisheries was directly involved in fishing and production, this was seen by the government as a temporary role and that ultimately it should engage primarily in the transfer of expertise. A joint Sudan Government/UNDP-FAO Fisheries Training Institute at Malakal was expected initially to undertake in service training for departmental staff but later the emphasis would be on training and producing fishermen.

The importance of fisheries exploitation cannot be over-emphasised. Considerable areas of the Region that lie within the tsetse belt, or are too far removed from permanent sources of water, lack animal protein. These areas could benefit from increased fish production. Amongst riverain tribes fish is an important component of diet, particularly during the dry season.

To conclude, it is important to point out some of the constraints to development during this period. The first obvious limitation to increased agricultural production was the unreliability of rainfall, leading either to drought or flooding. Agricultural methods and tools (mainly hand-hoes) were inadequate for the realisation of increased agricultural output as envisaged by the Six-Year Plan. Less than 2 percent of the land was under mechanised cultivation.[56] Ox-ploughing offered an intermediate technology which was well within the Region's financial and manpower resources, but its adoption required training and extension.

Pests and diseases often reach epidemic proportions and wipe out crops and herds. Any effort to increase yields or to introduce new crops required a wide range of plant protection activities. The introduction of sugarcane in Melut and Mongalla, for example, necessitated measures against the African locust. Certain birds are a menace to dura crops in particular, and all grain crops in general. Coffee trees need protection against berry borers.

Agriculture was and still is basically for subsistence; there was little or no incentive for the farmer to produce more by adopting new methods, especially when the latter almost always entailed large capital inputs. Most farmers were still outside the modern monetary economy. To bring these farmers into the economy would entail a major change in their way of life. Perhaps a wide-spread extension service could have made this possible, though it would have required considerable ingenuity and patience on the part of the extension officers as well as the establishment of an efficient system of communications, control and monitoring of operations. In more advanced countries an extension service acts more as a distribution and service unit between producers of scientific knowledge and the farmer. In the Southern Region however, the extension service was first designed to create in the farmer a desire to change and improve his methods. Only when the farmer wanted to enter the monetary market-oriented economy would the extension worker be able to help him. In all, this would have involved a comprehensive and delicate task and extension workers would have had to be trained accordingly.

Animal Wealth

The livestock industry also provided a basis for economic development. Due to the first civil war, little was done to control and eradicate epizootic diseases of livestock and no efforts were made to introduce modern management and marketing of surplus.

While accurate statistics of the livestock sector are not available, an estimate made by the International bank for Reconstruction and Development[57] based on hides and skins trading, provincial and district reports from JP15[58] vaccination campaign and previous estimates, placed the total livestock population at 9.6 million head (5.1 million cattle, 1.8 million sheep and 2.7 million goats). This figure is almost double that provided by the Southern Development Investigation Team in 1955. Additional estimates have indicated that the calf weaning rate was about 30 percent and adult mortality was about 1 0 percent. The off-take rate was estimated to be 2.5 to 3 percent per annum. "A rough estimate of trade in hides and skins puts the figure at 40,000 pieces per annum exported."[59]

Government plans for the development of the livestock industry were quite ambitious. These included control and eradication of the major epizootic diseases; increase in livestock production to achieve an exportable surplus; provision of milk to the urban centres and areas with no cattle; raising the quality of cattle and sheep; improving the quality of hides and skins for export; establishing livestock marketing organisations and arresting deterioration of grazing land by encouraging better management practices. The Regional Government also hoped to develop a beef industry.

Equally ambitious were the ways and means of attaining the above aims. A large scale vaccination programme was got under way in order to reduce mortality and morbidity as a precondition for the development of cattle exportation. In addition, the World Bank was assisting in the provision of mobile veterinary units backed up by diagnostic facilities. The problem however, was lack of adequate trained manpower and the chronic transport difficulties prevalent all over the region and in particular in the Nilotic areas. There were two dairy units, one in Juba and the other in Malakal. The World Bank planned to build three more. As regards sheep breeding, the Southern Region was less suited than the drier regions of the North. Many sheep died at the beginning of the rainy season, as happened, for example in Kongor in the Jonglei Canal area in April, 1975. Moreover the sheep are generally of a poorer quality than those in the North. Thus, efforts to introduce better breeds of rams into the existing flocks and to reduce losses from disease were initiated. A 4,000 acre Sheep Scheme was established at Kopoeta as a pilot unit for further expansions to other parts.

The poultry industry barely existed. Village level production had been severely disrupted by widespread epidemics of Newcastle disease and, if production was to survive, a widespread vaccination programme was necessary. Three units (in Juba, Wau and Malakal), each capable of producing 10,000 chicks per annum of improved breeds, were to be established. A major complex in Juba was planned for the production of 4 million eggs and 500,000 carcasses per year.

Despite the ambitious plans for the development of the livestock resources, the situation had hardly changed from what it was in the period prior to independence. However, in general, the aim of the Regional Government was mainly to raise the productivity of this sector and to increase the commercial off-take to meet demand in other parts which had little or no livestock (e.g. the tsetse infested areas).

Industry and Trade

Industrial development in the South has its natural base in agro-industries and in building material industries. The reactivation and expansion of industries based on cotton, coffee, tea and other crops for the domestic and also export markets could create considerable employment.

Unfortunately, little can be said about industrial growth for the simple reason that most of the old industries were yet to be reactivated fully and the new ones were still at the planning stage or under implementation. The Six-Year Plan (1977/78–1982/83) provided an impressive list of both Central Government and Regional Government financed projects. It remained to be seen whether these could have been realised. We can, however, make some general remarks about the industrial scene by discussing some of the problems faced in the implementation of industrial projects. Ideally, one would have preferred to make a detailed analysis of the performance of each industry or firm, but that would require precise data which is unavailable.

There was a spinning and weaving factory in Anzara and another at Mongalla. The Anzara factory was reopened in 1970 but was only operating at half capacity because of lack of cotton which came from the Nuba Mountains by rail to Wau and by road.[60] The factory at Mongalla was opened in 1976 and likewise was not operating to its full capacity. On our way to Kongor in April, 1981, we found that the factory at Mongalla had been closed for four months because there was no cotton to spin and weave. The employees continued to receive their salaries, though not working, until cotton arrived from Kosti by steamer. The manager of the Anzara Spinning and Weaving Mill complained that work came to a standstill every year for four to six months largely because of lack of cotton which was not available locally in sufficient quantity.

Two other industrial projects for Mongalla were included in the Six-Year Plan. The first was the reopening of the old Mongalla Sugar Factory which had been closed down in the early sixties by the military regime of General Abboud. In early July, 1981, when we last visited Mongalla, this project had not yet been implemented. The main reason given by the officials of the Regional Ministry of Agriculture in Juba was that the machinery for the factory could not be transported from Port Sudan to Mongalla on time, and, even when some parts arrived, there would always be the problem of lack of finance or working capital. Finance was not always forthcoming from Khartoum even if approval for it had been made in the Budget.

Another industrial project was the Mongalla Agro-Industrial Complex which was financed by the Government of the Netherlands. This complex included a dairy farm and milk production and processing unit; a chicken and egg farm; a saw mill and a fruit processing plant. We visited this complex in May 1981 and, apart from the construction of the saw mill building and the arrival of the machinery for milk processing and incubators (which were lying in the sun along the bank of the Bahr el Gebel), the project had not yet been completed. It is worth noting that the Southern Sudanese manager for the Mongalla Agro-Industrial Complex blamed the Dutch for not fulfilling their part of the contract, while in a report[61] to the Regional Government, the Dutch tended to emphasise the transport difficulties and the slow bureaucratic procedures they had to deal with in Juba.

A new sugar factory was planned at Melut as well as the reopening of the one at Mongalla. The Melut Sugar Project was a central government undertaking. Sugarcane was planted with some success. However, the actual production of sugar had not yet started. Thus, sugar, which is an important commodity, was not produced in the South and still had to be imported from the North.

One of the few industrial projects that had been operating with some success was the Wau Fruit Canning Factory, which had been producing canned fruits and vegetables (e.g. okra, mangoes, pineapples and oranges) for about ten years. The factory was established by the Russians in early 1972 and the fruit processed was transported to it from Western Equatoria. Its products were already being sold all over the country, though at certain times in the year the quantities of fruit available was small and production fell considerably. The shortages of fruit were caused either because of transport difficulties or because of crop failures in Western Equatoria. When fruit was not available the factory reverted to producing cans of Egyptian beans (imported from the North) or even beef.

There were a number of old saw mills in Katire, Gilo, Lanya, etc., which were established during the pre-independence period and were being revived by the Regional Government. The fact that the Regional Government still referred to the need to reactivate these saw mills showed that these were not yet fully operational.[62]

Private sector involvement in industry was minimal. The Haggar Group of Companies produced several brands of cigarettes in Juba using tobacco from its farms in the Yei area. In addition, there was a soft-drinks factory in Juba that produced several thousand bottles per month, but these were not sufficient to meet the demand of Juba town which was then estimated to have a population of over 50,000 people. Perhaps the most significant private sector participation in industry was that of bakery businesses in the towns. There were ten bakeries in Juba alone and at least one in each of the major towns. This private sector participation was controlled by the *Jellaba* or Northern Sudanese traders. Few Southerners had entered into industrial activities, largely due to lack of finance capital.

To further illustrate the industrial and trade situation let us examine in some detail two parastatal organisations under the Regional Government; namely the Regional Development Corporation (RDC) and the Equatoria Trading Corporation (ETC). The RDC was established soon after the Addis Accord to promote industrial growth as well as creating a favourable atmosphere for agriculture (largely through credit) and trade. The corporation operated a number of companies such as the Yirol Oil Mill, established in 1975, but this had not yet made any noticeable progress. A Sudanese Italian Tourist Company was also established with an operating capital of one and a half million Sudanese Pounds (L.S.1.5 million), 25 percent of which constituted the share of the RDC. The other partners were the Central Government (50 percent) and the Italians (25 percent). The company operated two tourist villages, one at Arous near Port Sudan and the other at Gimeiza near Mongalla in Eastern Equatoria. Though no figures are available to show the company's performance, it was nevertheless rated as highly profitable (at least by the officials of the RDC). A Regional Insurance Company had also been established from a partnership of the RDC (51 percent share), General Insurance Co., Khartoum (35 percent) and the National Re-Insurance Co., Khartoum (14 percent). Again there are no statistics by which to assess performance.

A more ambitious project of the RDC was started at Rotun, just on the northern outskirts of Juba Town, as a mixed farm for dairy, poultry, piggery and crop production. In the 1975 season 200 feddans were sown with maize. Production was satisfactory as tractors and fertilisers were used. The main difficulty faced was flooding caused by the adjacent Luri River. In the same year, two bulls and 50 Freisian heifers in calf were imported from Kenya and a good number of them calved soon after arrival. However, the dairy and poultry products from Rotun met only some of the demand of the large civil service and trading communities in Juba. These products were scarce and the vast majority of the town dwellers had no access to them.

Another area of the RDC's activities was that of providing agricultural and small commercial loans to the public. The picture in this respect looked as in Table 6 for 1974–1975 Fiscal Year.

The credit facilities as showed in Table 6 were intended for small farmers and traders as well as for rural co-operative societies. We have reason to believe that sizeable amounts of these funds went to big traders or were used by bureaucrats to purchase cattle for personal acquisition. Most of the applications for credit approved in Equatoria (i.e. 174 applications approved) went to persons resident in Juba and not to small farmers in rural areas. Probably the same was true in the case of Bahr el Ghazal and Upper Nile provinces, which in any case received

Table 6. *Number of Applications for Agricultural and Commercial Loans.*

Province	No. Applications Received	No. Applications Approved	Sum Allotted (Sterling Pounds)
Equatoria	301	174	41,682
B/Ghazal	163	47	10,118
Upper Nile	38	19	5,800
TOTAL	502	240	65,100

Source: "Peace and Progress", Regional Ministry of Information and Culture, Juba, 1977.

less than half the sum allotted for such credit. Furthermore, tight conditions over collateral security (often arbitrarily decided by the officials of RDC) for eligibility, often disqualified small farmers and Southern Sudanese traders. Out of the 174 approved applications for credit in Equatoria, 149 went to coffee growers who happened to be top level civil servants or sometimes Ministers, not to the small coffee farmers in Yei District or Gilo areas in Eastern Equatoria.[63]

The second public corporation is the Equatoria Trading Corporation (ETC). The old Equatoria Projects Board (EPB) consisted of two sister branches, the Trading Division and the Production Division. In 1970, the EPB was abolished and the ETC was created from the Trading Division, while the Production Division was annexed to the National Agricultural Production Corporation. The task of the ETC was to promote the commercial sector; import vital consumer goods not locally produced or in short supply; undertake wholesale distribution of these essential commodities and also control prices. To date, the ETC has not had much success in its major tasks and least of all in controlling prices. In Table 7 some of the commodities imported to the Region over the period 1972 to 1976 are shown.

The fall in imports was not because of a growth in local production but, in reality, reflects the increasing lack of finance faced by the corporation as well as the chronic inefficiency in transporting these commodities. In addition, despite the Corporation's almost total monopoly of imports (including sugar, which was not included in the table), private traders had stepped up "smuggling" of these commodities which they were forbidden by law to import. Only the corporation was legally entitled to import them and sell them to traders or to the public directly. In most cases the commodities imported by the ETC were bought wholesale by traders, hoarded for a time in order to create an artificial shortage, and then sold later at 'black market prices'.

Table 7. *Commodities Imported to the South (1972–1976)*

Commodity	1972	1973	1974	1975	1976
Wheat-flour (bags)	194,763	142,971	33,720	36,009	4,710
Grain (bags)	193,620	78,219	51,615	48,921	66,720
Rice (bags)	4,770	7,938	930	2,091	300
Lentils (bags)	2,391	2,655	750	300	150
Salt i) (bags)	8,257	5,968	4,928	2,120	4,131
ii)(cartons)	9,800	1,500	2,999	700	–

Source: "Six-Year Plan ...", Juba, 1977.

The trading pattern was conditioned by the fact that production activities were fragmented in small units with low overall volume of output. In addition, the transport system was poor. This inhibited the easy flow of goods from point to point in an exchange market. Trading by local petty traders to local clients and some barter trade had long been prevalent, but it was dominated by a few traders: it was almost always Northern Sudanese at the main town centres who operated a network of 'bush' shops scattered about population agglomerates in rural areas. The rural shops were also collecting points for the produce of the surrounding area.

While theoretically this system should have acted as a stimulant to economic development, trading continued to be a passive, rather than an active, component of economic activity. Production in the rural areas continued to be in small scattered units with low volume of production per unit, as well as deficiencies in infrastructural facilities like transport, storage and financing to support production and marketing. Under the circumstances the volume of trade did not increase in step with the requirements for accelerated development. The traders, with their near monopoly of basic consumer goods, were usually content with their large margin of profit. Comparing their position to that of fellow Northerners who migrated to the oil-rich Middle East countries in search of quick riches, a *Jellaba* trader remarked that "their Kuwait or Saudi Arabia is the South where they could make large profits in a short time through trade."[64] The *Jellaba* had not then felt it worthwhile to reinvest their profits in industry; least of all to undertake 'risky' investments in agriculture. It is impossible to estimate how much profit these traders made, but it almost always found its way back to the North.

There were Unity Bank branches in almost all the provincial capitals, but since these were commercial banks, they did not generally lend money to the public, except in the case of traders who satisfied their tight credit conditions; most deposits (particularly savings) were channelled back to the parent bank in Khartoum. The specialised banks (the Agricultural, Industrial and Estates banks) had no branches in the South and so credit which could have been forthcoming from these banks was not available. Furthermore, the lack of confidence of the Northern traders in the stability of the peace arrangement between the North and the South, prevented them from reinvesting commercial profits made in the South in industry. Whereas the Regional Government might have been able to plan and direct investment as well as encourage trade, it had no means at its disposal to control or even determine the level of savings in the economy beyond revenues it collected.

Power

Public electricity supply was by and large confined to Juba, Wau and Malakal, all was generated from small diesel-powered equipment installed in the 1950s and 1960s. The installed capacities at these centres were as follows:

Table 8. *Electricity Supply*

Location	Number of Units	Capacity/KW
Juba	8	920
Wau	6	600
Malakal	5	840

Source: "Six-Year Plan for Social and Economic Development in the Southern Region, 1977/78–1982/83", Juba, June 1977.

Additional generating capacity was installed in Bor, Yambio and Rumbek. Generally, the equipment in these centres needed replacement or substantial renovation. The distribution facilities were inadequate and incapable of meeting the growing demand for electricity in these towns, either for domestic or commercial and industrial use. Except for a small hydro-electric plant at Katire, which was used to power the saw mill, hydro-electricity potential had not been utilised. The stretch of the Bahr el Gebel between Nimule and Juba, an area where almost the entire regional potential is located, has a theoretical potential at low water of between 1,000 Megawatts (MW) in a good year and 500 MW in an exceptionally low year.[65] Three possible locations for hydro-electric projects were partially surveyed. That at Fola had a potential of 97 MW, Makedo 22 MW and Beden 22 MW. The location of Beden had a preferred status due to its relative proximity to Juba and Mongalla, which were important consumption centres. No other areas of high potential existed in the Region, even if small hydro-electric generators could have been operated on some of the other rivers. These, however, had not yet been surveyed.

Transport and Communication

The road system was developed as complementary to the river transport system. The transport and communications network was largely the same as that which existed prior to independence. In the absence of precise information on distances of both seasonal and all-weather roads, the following table of distance of various points in the South from Khartoum and Port Sudan, provides a guide to both the remoteness of the area and the difficulties of internal transport and communications. The great distance from the main internal market and the seaport must be considered together with great natural obstacles to communication such as the vast Sudd Region. Roads in the Central Rainlands and Flood Zones were constructed for the convenience of the administration system and to interconnect the major population centres. They run mainly along the water courses. Roads in the Central Rainlands were comparatively easily constructed by bush and grass clearing and grading. The flood zone roads required embankments, small bridges and culverts. However, in these zones the roads are almost impassible during the rainy season. The figures in Table 9 speak for themselves.

In the Equatorial Zone roads were built to connect the main centres with the river system. The road system, therefore, originally radiated from such ports as Wau, Meshra er Req, Shambe and Juba These roads were maintained as all-weather roads with permanent bridges. These have been well designed and constructed and have the advantages of good terrain and ecological conditions. However, through lack of maintenance during the first civil war period and the destruction of bridges by the 'freedom fighters', the road system in these areas had degenerated and was still being upgraded in many sections.

Table 9. *Distance of Various Points in the Southern Provinces from Khartoum and Port Sudan along the Existing Lines of Communication in Miles. (Distance by Rail Kosti-Khartoum = 238 Miles)*

Locality	Khartoum			Port Sudan
	Road	River	Total	Total
Renk		108	364	807
Malakal		311	549	1,011
Nasir	130	311	679	1,140
Boma via Bor	253	787	1,278	1,749
Rumbek via Shambe	115	457	810	1,271
Wau		708	946	1,407
Raga	207	708	1,153	1,614
Juba		892	1,130	1,591
Kapoeta	194	892	1,324	1,785
Yambio	323	892	1,453	1,914
Source Yubo	464	892	1,594	2,055

Source: Basinski, J. J., "Some Problems of Agricultural Development in the Southern Provinces of the Sudan", in Sudan Notes and Records, Nos. 37–39, 1956–58, n. 27.

After the Addis Ababa Accord of 1972, the need to link the Southern Region with Mombasa and the East African Region to enable quicker and easier transport added an extra dimension to the rationale of road building. Roads connecting Juba with Nimule and with Kenya through Kapoeta gained importance in transport planning. Additionally, the need for linking the various parts of the Region to stimulate the growth of production and trading activities provided a strong incentive for a co-ordinated programme of upgrading all main roads and constructing a network of feeder roads. The road transport services were almost entirely operated by private enterprise (mainly Northern Sudanese business concerns), except for official transport on government account; while the river, air and railway systems were state monopolies. Road transport between important population and commercial centres was operated largely with lorries and trucks owned by small fleet owners as well as by single-unit operators. Considering the fact that the road system was not particularly satisfactory the transport operatives fulfilled a vital function quite creditably. They widened their operations in the ten years after 1972 to the extent that Juba was connected to the East African countries by road through regular operations of international trucking companies and individual operatives owned by Sudanese (mostly not Southerners) and foreigners.

The river transport system which was in the past the only link between the North and the South, as well as the only link between Juba and the important centres along the White Nile in the Sudd area, has a unique role insofar as land transportation in this zone is impractical for a large part of the year. For example, the implementation of the Melut and Mongalla Sugar factories and the Mongalla Agro-Industrial Complex, depended on the efficiency of the river system. The system, however, had been in a poor condition for years. The main reasons for the poor state of the river system were the inadequate port facilities, the condition of the aged river crafts, lack of repair facilities for boats except in Khartoum North and the worsening navigational problems in the river due to the growth of water hyacinth in all the Southern Reach (i.e. from Kosti to Juba). However, despite deficiencies, the system continued to be vital to the Region for commercial links with the North.

The Sudan Railway line operating into Wau is the only rail link between North and South. This served a vital function in freight transport to Bahr el-Ghazal and Lakes provinces. For example, when local raw material (fruit and vegetables) were not available at certain times of the year, Egyptian broad beans for the Wau Canning Factory had to be transported from the North by rail. Cotton for the Anzara Spinning and Weaving Factory came from the Nuba Mountains by rail to Wau and then by road to Anzara. The rail link to Wau was also important for passenger transport.

Sudan Airways operations to Juba, Wau and Malakal from Khartoum and to Nairobi through Juba, are of critical importance for both passenger and freight traffic. The traffic has been sharply increasing in recent years so that there are now daily flights to the South from Khartoum. However, it is not uncommon for the South to be cut off from the rest of the country for many months in a year due to either the bad condition of airports (especially runways) or due to the usual lack of aviation fuel in these airports or even in Khartoum itself. At present the war hinders all normal means of transportation and communication.

Chapter 4

The Position of South Sudan Within the Sudan Economy

The South is poorer and less developed than the rest of the country. The South depends on the North for much of the finance required for its development efforts. We must, however, recognise that some parts of the North (e.g. Kordofan, Darfur and Red Sea areas) can be regarded as equally poor and underdeveloped. The recent creation of regions within the North (based mainly upon the model adopted for the South in 1972 following the Addis Ababa Agreement) is partly a recognition of this fact.

Table 10 shows the regional distribution of manufacturing industries in the Sudan in 1970/71; it can be seen that most of the manufacturing establishments are concentrated in Khartoum, Blue Nile and Kassala provinces. The Southern Provinces together had only one manufacturing firm (i.e. Wau Fruit Canning Factory) and the lowest value added of manufacturing products and level of employment, with the exception of Darfur. The three rich provinces of Khartoum, Blue Nile and Kassala are responsible for 91.9 percent and 93.3 percent of investment resources and value added in manufacturing, as well as 90 percent of the total industrial production. Except for a few industrial establishments (e.g. the Nzara and Mongalla Cotton Mills and Saw Mills) the Southern Provinces still have very few such enterprises and these, we have seen earlier, are hampered by transport difficulties, lack of spare parts and lack of finance.

Table 11 shows that the First National Five Year Plan (1970/71–1976/77) allocated 24.6 percent of agricultural and irrigational resources to the Southern Region. Resources allocated for industry and mining were slightly higher (26.5 percent). These very high percentages (compared to those for the Northern Provinces except Khartoum) reflect the intention of the Central Government to allocate more development resources to the Southern Region which had just emerged from seventeen years of civil war. However, as we have seen earlier, these resources have not actually been made available. As so often, allocating resources through a plan does not in itself mean that the actual flow of these resources will take place. As we shall discuss later, the actual realisation of planned targets has not been so successful, due largely to

Table 10. *Regional Distribution of Manufacturing Industries (1970/72)*

Province	Establish-ment		Total prod.		Value added		Employ-ment		Total wages		Total investment	
	No.	%	000'	%	000'	%	No.	%	000s	%	000'	%
Khartoum	153	73.3	54144	66.1	16885	61.5	27653	4.6	8693	647.2	48451	47.2
Blue Nile	18	8.6	13319	16.3	5232	19.1	8541	19.9	1850	14.3	24935	24.3
Kassala	13	6.2	10398	12.7	3772	13.7	4161	9.7	1691	13.0	20688	20.4
Northern	5	2.4	2146	2.6	859	3.1	1140	2.7	379	2.9	4575	4.4
Kordofan	16	7.7	1366	1.7	545	2.0	928	2.2	202	1.6	2661	2.6
Darfur	3	1.4	157	0.2	31	0.1	134	0.3	10	0.1	170	0.2
Southern Province	1	0.5	362	0.4	127	0.5	263	0.6	122	0.9	924	0.9
TOTAL	209	100.0	81892	100.0	27451	100.0	42823	100.0	12947	100.0	102704	100.0

Source: "Plans for Industrial Development in Sudan", Ministry of Industry and Mining, Khartoum, 1974.

Table 11. *Regional Allocation of Investments According to Sectors in the Amended Five-Year Plan (1970/71–1976/77) in Sudanese Pounds*

Provinces	Agriculture & irrigation		Industry & mining		Transport & communi-cation		Services	
	000s	%	000s	%	000s	%	000s	%
Khartoum	7004	2.3	17415	6.0	30242	15.5	39538	83.5
Blue Nile	12800	41.9	118960	40.8	40078	20.6	7123	6.6
Kassala	55404	18.1	31333	10.7	104242	54.0	482	1.0
Northern	15750	5.1	35579	12.2	1687	0.8	850	1.8
Kordofan	13283	4.1	5700	1.9	5540	2.9	271	0.6
Darfur	10203	3.3	5700	1.9	10416	5.4	62	0.1
Southern Region	75290	24.6	76800	26.5	1944	1.0	3017	6.4
Sub Total	305034	100.0	291487	100.0	194149	100.0	47343	100.0
Unclassified	20000		282424		12337		87054	
GRAND TOTAL	325034		303911		206476		134397	
Actual Exp.	166228		135261		136361		90362	

Source: Ministry of Planning and National Economy, Democratic Republic of the Sudan, "The Amended Five-Year Plan for Economic and Social Development (1970/71–1976/77), The Phased Action Programme, Estimation of Development Budget", pp. 37–70.

structural difficulties in the financial relationship between the Central Government and the Regional Government in Juba.

Table 11 also shows that in the field of transport and communications (which form major constraints to development), the South received only 1 percent of the resources allocated. The plan also provided 6.4 percent of total investments of services for the South. This is a very low figure, considering the requirements for reconstruction and rehabilitation following the 1972 Peace Agreement.

The distribution of output and employment in agriculture also shows a trend towards regional imbalance; but again with the Southern Provinces being very much at the bottom of the table. Table 12 shows that the Southern Provinces together produced only 11.8 percent of the total (in 1973/74) of the combined value of main crops and animal produce. However, this figure may be misleading in that it includes only the value of the marketed surplus and excludes the total value of the output of the large traditional sector. Even allowing for this the South has the lowest agricultural output. Perhaps this is so because in the North rain-fed cultivation is supplemented by irrigation in large mechanised schemes which do not exist in the South. The figures also serve albeit indirectly, to illustrate the extent of the differences in incomes derived from agricultural activities in the various provinces, since agriculture is the main source of income. The IL0 Mission Report (1976), from which the table below was taken, put the national average *per capita* income at Sudanese Pounds 65, but only Sudanese Pounds 30 in the South.

The South also lags behind in education and health facilities, which were virtually non-existent during the civil war period. The ILO Mission (1976) estimated that in 1973/74 there were 10 health centres, 97 dispensaries and 218 dressing stations in the South, compared to 128, 523 and 1671 respectively in the North. This discrepancy still prevails. Up to 1972 there were only two Senior Secondary schools in the South compared to over forty such institutions in the North.[66] During the civil war, most of the intermediate and primary schools were closed down and the two senior secondary schools were relocated in the North. The situation improved greatly. In the 1980/81 academic year, there was a total of 748 primary schools, 92 intermediate schools and 19 senior secondary schools.[67] In addition, the University of Juba was opened in September 1977 as the first institution of higher learning in the Region. However, despite this remarkable improvement in educational facilities, the South remains relatively backward. For example, the opening of one University in Juba was followed by a University in the Gezira, and three others (El Obeid, El Fasher and Kassala) are being created in the North. This is in addition to the already existing 26 institutions of higher learning in the North.[68]

Other services, like post and telegraph offices, are few. According to the 1976 ILO Mission Report, there were only 26 post and telegraph offices in the South, while the Northern Provinces had 178 such offices.

The Six-Year Plan for the Southern Region (1977/78–1982/83) was the first major step towards correcting the trend towards unequal development. Let us, therefore, examine in some detail the aims and the new strategy for the development of the South as laid down in that plan.

Table 12.* *Regional Distribution of Output and Employment in Agriculture*

PROVINCE	PERCENTAGES		
	Value of main crops	Combined value of main crops and animal outputs	Agricultural working population
Kassala	14.6	17.0	4.5
Blue Nile	55.6	38.1	22.1
Darfur	6.5	11.6	23.0
Kordofan	17.6	18.0	19.3
Equatoria	1.4	1.9	6.2
Bahr el Ghazal	1.9	5.2	12.1
Upper Nile	2.0	4.7	7.3

**Note*: Khartoum and Northern Provinces are excluded and so the totals have not been made since these would not add up to 100.

Source: ILO, "Growth,. Employment and Equity...", 1976.

Chapter 5

Development Planning: the Six-Year Plan for the Southern Region (1977/78–1982/83)

In spite of past efforts to establish such projects as the Zande Scheme and other agricultural and forestry schemes, no comprehensive plan for the social and economic development of the South was ever undertaken prior to the 1972 Peace Accord. Until then the Southern Sudan was isolated and neglected by its various rulers. The peace agreement of 1972 created the conditions conducive to a reversal, or at least the arresting, of this state of 'underdevelopment'. These new conditions were the establishment of peace and stability, resettlement of refugees and displaced persons, rehabilitation and reconstruction of the social and economic infrastructure. As well as establishing new machinery for self-rule, the new Regional Government started laying the foundations of a system of public finance and budgetary control. The present three Regions in the South formed after the re-division of the southern Regional Government in 1983 follow the same system.

The Southern Region's budgetary system consists of a recurrent and a development budget, in line with that found in the Central Government. As there were few public or private enterprises, the coverage of these budgets was limited to the Southern Regional Government. The salient features of the two budgets were:

a) The almost complete dependence of Southern Regional Government on the Central Government for the major proportion of its revenue; and
b) The 'fixed' nature of the major part of the Central Government transfers to Southern Regional Government; and the possibility of only a very slow growth of revenues under the variable items.

All recurrent expenditures, other than those reserved for the Central Government by the Accord, were included in the Southern Regional Government's budget. However, the Southern Regional Government's special development budget covered only part of the total development expenditures, since the Central Government development budget provided for those projects in the Region which were centrally planned and executed, for example the Jonglei Canal Project.

In addition to Southern Regional Government's budgets there were provincial budgets for each of the six provinces. These provincial budgets and those of the local councils within their jurisdiction depended heavily on transfers from the Central Government via Southern Regional Government, but they included some local revenue as well. Southern Regional Government's approval was required for the provincial budgets, and it had the responsibility of making up for any deficits in them. However, as concluded by an IBRD (International Bank for Reconstruction and Development) report, the Southern Regional Government "had indicated its unwillingness to cover such deficits".[69]

Generally, financial flows between the Central Government and the Southern Regional Government (including the provincial and local councils) can be summarised by the diagram below. Our subsequent discussion of development planning will further illustrate this aspect of Southern Regional Government-Central Government relationship.

The Addis Accord (1976)[70] specified that planning for economic and social development was a Central Government function. Consequently, the Central Government expenditures in the whole Sudan, including the South, were Khartoum's concern. However, Southern Regional Government was empowered to prepare a supplemental special development budget. Hence the First Six-Year Plan for the South was initiated in 1977/78 to last till the financial year 1982/83.[71] The Six-Year Plan for the South stated its long term objectives as "raising the standard of living of the people to the highest level and providing opportunities for gainful employment to all in the labour force in a society based on the principles of social justice and individual freedom".[72] A number of other platitudes followed, but these need not detain us here. It is important to note that the Plan did not envisage the construction of new projects, but rather laid emphasis on the improvement of the then existing ones and their intensification through better management, technical production and marketing improvement etc., in order to maximise output. This contrasted sharply with policy so far as the Jonglei Canal was concerned.

The strategy of development laid down in the plan gave priority to agriculture, animal production, forestry and fisheries, since these primary producing sub-sectors are regarded as the keys to Southern economic growth. To achieve this, "priority will be given to pushing the traditional producers to move forward to increased *per capita* output and generation of additional employment".[73] The Plan also recognised the need to improve and expand transport and communications facilities.

Table 13. *Six-Year Development Plan 1977/78--982/83 Approved Financial Allocation by Sector (Regional Resources) (in Sudanese Pounds)*

S/No.	Sector	1977/78–1982/83	1977/78	1978/79	1979/80	1980/81	1981/82	1982/83
1	Agri-culture	25,583,734	5,265,214	4,193,184	4193184	3,879,942	2,808,851	5,356,602
2	Industry	26,766,644	5,837,457	5,110,141	4,768,125	4,035,831	3,695,421	3,319,669
3	Trans-port	29,066,046	3,844,572	7,172,683	7,059,532	4,611,332	3,443,798	2,934,129
4	Service	149,893,576	17,542,757	23,089,139	25,566,586	25,955,275	26,307,719	31,432,100
	TOTAL	231,310,000	32,490,000	39,451,904	41,587,427	38,141,970	36,596,199	43,042,500

Table 14. *Six-Year Development Plan 1977/78–1982/83 Approved Financial Allocation by Ministry and Sector 1977/78–1982/83 (in Sudanese Pounds)*

S/no.	Regional Ministry	Total 1977/78–82/83	%	SECTOR			
				Agriculture	Industry	Transport	Services
1	Agriculture	37,117,478	16.1	21,684,043	38,858,076	400,000	11,175,359
2	Commerce	3,439,807	1.5	–	1,718,585	–	1,721,222
3	Communi-cations	43,841,744	19.0	–	811,000	28,486,046	14,544,698
4	Cooperatives	15,000,000	6.5	197500	6,392,310	18,000	8,230,190
5	Education	15,258,699	6.6	–	558,000	–	14,700,699
6	Finance	64,039,649	27.7	–	2,199,481	–	63,819,668
7	Health	16,127,960	7.0	–	1,648,490	–	14,479,470
8	Housing	10,417,896	4.5	–	3,747,902	–	6,669,994
9	Information	6,874,953	3.0	–	1,709,455	–	5,165,498
10	Public Service	1,577,889	0.7	–	130,100	–	1,447,789
11	Admini-stration	8,400,225	3.6	590105	5,292,545	–	2,517,575
12	Wildlife	8,000,000	3.5	3112086	276,500	–	4,611,414
13	Youth and Sports	1,213,700	0.5	–	403,700	–	810,000
	TOTAL	231,310,000	100.0	25,583,734	26,766,644	29,066,046	149,893,576

Source: "Six-Year Plan for the Economic and Social Development of the Southern Region", Juba, June , 1977.

The target growth rate was of the order of 4.5 to 7 percent per annum to be achieved by the end of the Plan period.

The above were the broad objectives. It is worthwhile looking at some of the details of the Plan's aspirations and the past performance of the regional economy in order to ascertain the likelihood of attaining the declared goals. The Plan incorporated projects that required a total outlay of Sudanese Pounds 288,267,874 for the whole period. For the sectoral allocation of this outlay, see tables 13 and 14.

Table 13 shows that the service sector took the bulk of the resources approved for the Plan. Table 14 shows too that the bulk of the resources (over Sudanese Pounds 63 million) of the finance allocated went to services controlled by the Regional Ministry of Finance. Perhaps this underlies the trend then towards the expansion of the Civil Service in general administration.

The Plan identified three sources of finance (Sudanese Pounds):

A. Regional Resources	231,310,000
B. Central Government Contributions to Special Projects	35,972,154
C. External Assistance	21,085.720
	288,267,874

Source: "Six-Year Plan ...", p. 52

The regional resources were to consist partly of surplus from the recurrent budget and partly from subvention from the Central Government. In addition to a subvention of Sudanese Pounds 180 million, the Central Government was to make a contribution of Sudanese Pounds 35,872,154 to various projects which would be implemented by the Regional Government.

There were, however, a number of Central Government projects which were part of the National Six-Year Plan (1977/78–1982/83) but were to be carried out in the Southern Region. Table 15 (derived from the National Six-Year Plan) shows the amounts allocated to the various sectors on which these Projects were to be implemented.

The amount of Sudanese Pounds 66,451,000 was for projects which included large-scale mechanised farming of rice, coffee and tea. It also included the amount allotted for agricultural research, tsetse fly eradication and an experimental Project for the production of raw material for paper manufacture. As we have mentioned earlier, the Aweil rice scheme was operating with some success; the Malakal rice scheme was almost at a standstill; and the coffee and tea projects were being revived with Central Government assistance. As for the manufacture of paper from papyrus in Upper Nile, the plan had not taken off beyond the establishment of an office in Malakal for experts employed for the purpose.

Table 15. *Central Government Projects in the Southern Region Approved in the National Six-Year Plan 1977/78–1982/83 by Sector*

Sector	No. of Projects	Amount Approved (1977/78–1982/83) in Sudanese Pounds
Agriculture	11	66,451,000
Industry	7	110,800,000
Transport	9	23,811,000
Services	10	7,413,704
TOTAL	37	208,475,704

Source: "The National Six-Year Plan, 1977/78–1982/83".

The industrial projects included in Table 15, such as the Kenaf Factory at Tonj, the Palm Oil Factory at Yirol and the Wau Brewery, had not yet started production. The Melut and Mongalla Sugar Complexes had also not been established. The only Central Government financed industrial project which was effectively established was the Mongalla Spinning and Weaving Factory, and even then it was often at a standstill.

A large part of the amount allotted to transport (i.e. Sudanese Pounds 15,000,000) was designated for the construction of an all-weather road between Juba and Lodwar in Kenya. This is a .vital link since imports via the port of Mombasa in Kenya take a shorter time to arrive than those from Port Sudan. This road was completed and plans were underway to asphalt it. The rest of the amount allotted for transport was earmarked for the reconstruction of bridges destroyed during the first civil war and improving the Southern Reach of the river transport system.

As for external assistance, the Plan aimed to acquire these resources from international agencies, voluntary organisations and through bilateral trade agreements. External assistance was to be committed to specific projects, for example the construction of the Juba-Bor road by the Dutch Degroot Company and the Shambe-Yirol and Rumbek-Wau roads by the Germans. Another example of foreign assistance was the

German Medical Team which supplied doctors to various hospitals and was also involved in disease control.

A look at the performance of the Regional Government in terms of revenue collection during its first five years of existence indicated the growth of revenue. Since the administrative and technical apparatuses of government were relatively young and weak, the available data is inadequate for forecasting the path of this growth. The following table (16) shows the performance of the Southern Regional Government in revenue collection during its first five years of life (i.e. 1973/74–1977/78).

Table 16. *Revenue from 1973/74 to 1977/78 (in Sudanese Pounds)*

Local Revenue	1973/74	1974/75	1975/76	1976/77	1977/78
Non-tax revenues	466,363	1,943,889	2,601,862	4,140,800	5,601,140
Tax revenues	–	2,728,500	3,156,236	4,627,436	8,427,400
Sub-total SRG revenues	466,363	4,672,389	5,758,098	8,768,236	14,028,540
Central govt. grants	550,000	10,991,050	15,000,,050	17,800,000	20,800,000
TOTAL	5,966,363	15,663,439	20,758,148	26,568,236	34,828,540

Source: "Six-Year Plan", p. 56.

Thus, the percentage growth in revenue in the various components of these revenues was as can be seen in Table 17. It is clear from this Table that the Southern Regional Government (and even the present structures built after 1983) was heavily dependent on Central Government Grants for the realisation of its planned development programmes. In addition, since both the taxation system and the administrative machinery that generated it were still at an infant stage and largely inefficient, the revenue projections of the plan might not have been fully realised. The awareness of the Regional Government of the dependence on Central Government finance, had in part led to the acceptance of, and the hope in, the Jonglei Scheme as a factor which would enable the Region to reduce this dependence.

Table 17. *Revenue from 1974/75 – 1977/78, Percentage Growth*

Fiscal Year	Tax Revenue	Non-Tax Revenue	Percentage Growth Central Govt. Grant	Total Revenue
1974/75	–	316	99	162
1975/76	15	33	36	32
1976/77	46	59	18	27
1977/78 (est.)	82	35	16	31

Source: "Six-Year Plan.....", p.56.

Not only do the present three Regions in the South share the same predicament as did the defunct SRG, but they do not even enjoy the hope laid in the Jonglei Scheme or any other. Their over-riding priorities are relief food and providing whatever security possible for their people.

Chapter 6

The Harvest of Agony: The Economy of War*

Background: War and Sudan's Socio-Economic Development Efforts

Sudan's development planning has been subjected to mounting pressures as a result of war which sparked political instability and continuous shifts of policy and orientation. It experienced two civil wars (1955–1972 and 1983 until today) and three military coups (1958–1964, 1969/1985 and 1989) since independence in 1956.

The Ten Year Plan 1961/1962–1970/1971 was overshadowed by the first civil war between the North and the South (1955/1972) and confronted severe shortages of trained manpower, lack of infrastructure and poor financial resources. The plan collapsed and was eventually abandoned in 1967. The next was the Five Year Plan 1970/1971–1974/1975 which was extended by an interim programme to continue until 1977. Although the plan had an impressive record of achievement during its initial period of implementation, it was confronted by severe financial and other constraints similar to those which confronted the Ten Year Plan. The Six Year Plan 1977/1986 was also ill-fated and experienced serious problems as early as 1977/1978. It suffered a huge increase in central Government expenditure, decrease in development aid and an unparalleled balance of payment deficit. These factors, among others, compelled the Sudan to join the IMF/World Bank structural adjustment programme. Hence 1982/1983–1984/1985 was announced as an austerity period. The economic hardship which the population experienced due to the lifting of the subsidies on basic commodities resulted in series of political unrests which eventually contributed to the fate of Numeirie's Government in April, 1985. The economic crisis coupled with the war in Southern Sudan encouraged the military to take over in June 1989.

*This chapter is reprinted with permission from M. A. Mohamed Salih *et al* (1989), Operation Life-Line, War Impacts on the Sudan, Inter-Africa Group, UNICEF, Nairobi.

In essence, political instability and the present war are among the main factors which have contributed to Sudan's economic problems. The situation since the war began in 1983 has been one of crisis management with no efforts to promote development. In fact the war interrupted production, transport, services and claimed the meagre infrastructure which existed in the South before the war. From now on the Sudan economy cannot be treated in any other manner than as a war economy, bearing in mind the serious consequences of such a predicament on an already malformed economic structure.

Effects of War on Production and Services

Agriculture

Efforts to achieve food security and transform the country into a net exporter of food to the Middle East was hampered by the 1983/1985 drought which affected about 7 million Sudanese. The decline in sorghum production, the main food in the country, required massive food relief supply to bridge the 1.5 mn. tons food gap in grain alone. In an agricultural based economy like the Sudan, the decline of food and cash crops production is a sign of an economic crisis with serious impacts on all sectors of the economy. The official figures are abstracts about food deficit and they do not point out who are the carriers of the burden of the food gap. Sudan was still an exporter of grain even during the famine period. The private owners of the large-scale mechanised schemes were still in a position to produce surplus grain for export.

The Southern regions (Equatoria, Bahr Al-Ghazal and Upper Nile) were not affected by drought and there were no floods in 1983/1985. There was however the war which displaced many people and prevented them from having access to their farms. This situation was aggravated as the war crept into the borders between the South and the North.

Although the agricultural sector revived in 1986 and continued to grow, mainly in the less affected modern rainfed large-scale mechanised schemes in the central rainlands, the war displaced about 4 million peoples and has threatened about 1.2 millions with starvation since 1987. Social life and food production among the small producers in and around the war zone is severely affected by the war. Population movement from the war zone to the urban centres was not regulated and many left their villages to live in relief camps in absolute poverty. With the total collapse of the agricultural sector in the South and the intensification of the war and the poor performance of the economy, the country became more and more dependent on massive food aid, such as Operation Life Line which began in late 1988.

Almost all the large scale production schemes in the war zone, whether under the government or the SPLA control, ceased to operate. This situation has led to the total collapse of the economy in the war zone and made it entirely dependent on commodities moved from other parts of the country or from abroad through relief organisations. The traditional production system, which depends mainly on agriculture and livestock sectors, virtually ceased to operate. One of the main reasons is that the farms are no longer accessible due to the planting of land mines. These have obstructed peoples movement out of their villages or the garrison towns to which they have been displaced. Mining of roads also led to a total paralysis of the transport system and hence no agricultural input can be advanced to those who need them in the war zone. Some villagers claim to have stopped their production activities because of the fear of having their crops taken by the rebels roaming the area. Grazing of animals has become also problematic since there is the risk of coming across land mines. In areas where nomads from other regions such as the Blue Nile, Kordofan and Darfur, used to move for part of the year and practice some symbiotic relation with the local population such activities have disappeared. Those nomads who still want to move in these areas do so without benefit of symbiotic relations. They also have to depend on the protection of their own militia and the government army or strike some form of agreements with the SPLA troops by which they provide these troops with food in exchange for the freedom to graze. Although no side of the warring parties would admit that such agreements exist, the nomads themselves acknowledge their existence and explain that it is the only way for their stock to survive—a small triumph for common sense.

As a result of the civil war most of the resources in rural areas have been subject to neglect and destruction. The rural environment can no longer support any population pressure and has gradually been marginalized. The traditional sector that characterises rural areas used to support the small and large urban centres in the region. This is no longer the case since no small scale cultivation can be steadily practised nor can cattle herding be maintained due to the lack of security. The rural population who used to maintain a reasonable subsistence level, and even exceed that to produce some surplus to satisfy some of the needs of urban dwellers in the region, have turned most of what used to be agriculturally productive or high potential grazing areas in the Southern region into a no-man-lands only frequented by SPLA members, government soldiers or armed militia. The ordinary citizens have been forced towards the centres held by SPLA, government held towns or fled the region altogether.

Indirectly related to the civil war in the South, but with similar impact, is the growing rural insecurity in parts of Western Sudan (Kordofan and Darfur), where rural life has been undermined by banditry and inter-ethnic conflicts. In certain parts of this area, for example, cattle rustling has reached such an extent that rural people are selling animals and moving out of the livestock economy. Cattle rustling seems to be going on in the SPLA held areas in Equatoria, Bahr El Ghazal and Upper Nile as well and the relations between ethnic groups remains extremely tense.

The magnitude of destruction of the economic resources can be seen from the number of projects that had to stop functioning in the primary sector. According to the final report of the National Dialogue Conference on Peace held in Khartoum Sept./Oct. 1989, (which represents the only up to date document on the issue) a large number of projects in the agricultural sector had to be suspended with a loss of substantial sums of money or in kind to both the region and the country as a whole. Reference here is particularly made to the large scale projects run by the regional government and donor organisations.

Industry

The share of manufacturing industry in the GDP is estimated at about 6 percent in 1989. The annual growth rate of this sector in 1983/1984 was 7.71 percent, but it dropped to 1.3 percent in 1988/1989 (Ministry of Finance, 1990). This was explained by the World Bank (1985 and UNIDO (1987) as a result of the under-utilisation of the capacity of manufacturing industry, which contributed negatively to the already poor performance of this sector. It was estimated by UNIDO in 1987 that the utilisation of manufacturing industry was between 60 percent and 70 percent in 1986 and by the World Bank (1985) only between 20 percent and 30 percent in 1987. However, it is difficult to establish a direct association between the war in the South and the decline of industrial production.

In general, continuous power failures, rationing of electricity for about 6 hours a day in the beginning of 1990, fuel shortages and other constraints have disrupted the performance of many factories and reduced their capacity to the minimum since the beginning of 1990. Furthermore, the diversion of foreign exchange from the purchase of raw material and spare parts to the war effort must have contributed adversely to the decline of export with negative impacts on the balance of payments as will be explained latter.

Mining

The growth rate of the mining sector in 1982/1983 was 30 percent, but due to the war situation it has declined to zero since 1987/1988. This also means that its share in the GDP has declined from over 3 percent to zero since the beginning of the war. This is mainly because production and geological surveys were halted and ongoing activities were abandoned. For example, gold mining operations which began in Kapoeta stopped even before the district fell under SPLA control in 1985.

The most significant impact of the war, however, can be seen with reference to the loss resulting from hindering the exploitation of the country's and the region's oil potential. Total, Shell and Sun Oil companies had to stop exploring, after having already achieved good results, due to the fact that areas where they were prospecting are now within the zone where the civil war renewed. By 1984 Chevron, which was almost ready to operate its oil fields, started to face security problems and had to withdraw its working force from the field by September 1985. It was planned that in early 1986 Chevron would start exporting 60,000 barrels á day, which could have earned the country a reasonable and extremely needed foreign exchange. Not only that, but even further losses were incurred because materials for the pipeline, which were already bought, had to be stored abroad at high costs. The estimated losses due to this delay in production is almost over two billion American dollars a day.

Transport

The growth rate of the transport system declined from 1.8 percent before the war to –3.3 percent in 1988/1989. This can be explained by the fact that transport between towns and villages within the war zone and between the North and the South was hardly functioning since the renewal of the war. Transport is largely confined to relief operations and the use of local means such as pack animals. Attempts made towards reaching trade and administrative centres in the South through rail and river transport are costly, since as early as 1983 most bridges were destroyed and rail tracks neglected because lack of security did not allow for servicing. A number exceeding 165 rail trucks and tankers have been waiting in Wau since 1983 subjecting the Railway Department to a loss of over 5 million Sudanese Pounds a year. The Railway Section between Babanusa and Aweil which is now used by Operation Lifeline is working at a very low capacity since it needs continuous maintenance. River transport has suffered many losses through attacks which forced the officials to suspend its regular operations from Juba in the South to

Kosti in the North by the end of 1984. Most of its equipment was held in towns between Malakal and Juba and being subjected to misuse and destruction.

Tourism

The tourism industry, which had started to contribute positively to the economy of the Southern Region since 1972, was hit hard by the civil war. The tourist village in Gummaza which started operating as a tourist attraction in 1976 was a target for an early attack by the rebel groups when the civil war was renewed. Equipment, buildings, furniture and cars were damaged and their estimated cost is over one billion Sudanese Pounds. In addition to the damage a revenue of US$ 700,000, representing the rent of the village which was paid in foreign currency, has been lost. The losses of Juba hotel since 1983 are estimated to 7,278,000 Sudanese Pounds. Over 150 tourist agencies ceased their tours operations which used to bring in about 45,000 tourists a year to the region. The revenue that such an industry could have given the country is estimated to be over US$ 600 million for the period 1983/89.

The impacts relate to the production activities in the public sector. It has already been mentioned that the traditional sector in rural areas, which is predominantly related to agricultural production, has been rendered ineffective. Neither the resources nor the manpower required for its operations are obtainable anymore and the destruction of the environment have made the utilisation of the land resources almost impossible. Private business and trade agencies in urban areas have suffered most and those who are able to move their business elsewhere have already done so. As far as the SPLA held areas are concerned some observers say that no activities for businessmen or trade agencies could be found. The economy does not even use currency and is more or less back to the ages of barter trade .

Development Projects in the War Zone

In view of the lack of reliable information on the war zone we can only point to the impact of the war on production through reviewing the position of the different economic projects that used to operate in the Southern Region prior to the renewal of the civil war in 1983. These projects cover the primary sector, secondary sector and the service sector and are executed by public institution, private or donor organisations. The performance of such projects during peace time may not be adequate in relation to the objectives that led to their establishment. However, they were in the process of getting the development process under way. To stop these projects from operating means retarding the development in the region and increasing the margin of inequality between the Southern Region and the rest of the country.

Among these is the Aweil Rice project whose target was to put 7,000 feddans under cultivation annually. The project is financed by the EEC and the Sudan Government with a total cost of 40.4 million Sudanese Pounds, 34 million of which was the contribution in foreign exchange. Only 700 feddan were put under production when the security situation in the area started to worsen and the numbers of the labour force started to fall. At present only 200 employees are taking part and the agricultural activities have been limited to the area in the proximity of the town.

The coffee production project in Equatoria which covered 12,000 feddans and produced up to 2,100 tons annually during the period 1978–83 is no longer operational. This is due to lack of security. Bahr el Ghazal milk production scheme had a similar fate when the foreign experts had to leave and 200 senior and junior staff members were dismissed after the beginning of the war. Still some 600 workers are kept on without any tasks to perform and get paid from the project funds. The tea plantation, the sawmill and other agricultural projects in Eastern Equatoria had to stop and some of them, like the forestry project which was funded by the European Development Fund costing up to US$ 47 million, had all its structure destroyed. All the semi-mechanised rainfed and irrigated schemes in the region have ceased functioning since 1983.

Other schemes which were to be financed by the UNDP or the World Bank in the area of rural development had to be abandoned, together with accompanying agricultural training institutes like the ones in Yei and Rumbek. The Norwegian Rural Development Project in Eastern Equatoria was also closed and the work on the Juba-Nairobi road had to stop.

A major project which could have had a significant impact on agricultural development in the South, the North and Egypt is the Jonglei Canal. The construction started by 1977 and it was supposed to finish by 1985. The objective was to secure a flow of 4.7 m. cubic meters that would be shared equally between Egypt and the Sudan. The immediate benefits for the region were to be the creation of an earth compacted road on the eastern side of the canal linking Malakal with Juba and the canal itself which should be navigable and reduce the distance between Malakal and Juba by 350 km. The local population should be able to use off-take water points for small irrigation projects and watering of their animals. By the time the construction stopped in February 1983 the expenditure on the project was approximately US$ 150 millions. The compensation paid to the international companies involved was US$ 17.1 million. In addition to this, large sums of money promised by donors were lost due to the delay of activities. Similar irrigation and agricultural projects faced the same destiny such as the Pinko Plain Project, Mongalla and Malut Sugar Factories, naming only a few. Other agricultural projects such as Tong and Mongalla factories have stopped since 1984 but their employees are still being paid.

The livestock sector has suffered tremendously. The Nuer, Dinka and other cattle owning groups of the South have had severe losses of herds. It is very difficult to give realistic estimates of such losses, but the report of the National Dialogue Conference for Peace suggests that the figure is in the proximity of 6.6 million heads of cattle.

As far as the wildlife is concerned the warring parties have been indiscriminate in their killing, forced by the need for food and (sometimes for commercial purposes). This has led to almost total destruction of the wildlife resources and the complete disappearance of some rare species.

The manufacturing sector in the South is small and was performing poorly even before the renewal of the civil war. The slow pace of development and progress in this sector was one of the main reasons fuelling the feeling of mistrust and suspicion. Even the limited efforts in this sector were halted by the renewal of the war.

A number of projects that started in the area of manufacturing had to cease production due to the lack of security in the area where the factories are established or where the raw materials came from. Self-sufficiency projects like the Anzara complex at which textile, soap, oil, sugar, coffee and other goods are produced was offered a grant of 2.5 million Kuwaiti Dinars for rehabilitation, but it was not possible to embark on such a task with the start of the war.

Wau Fruit and Vegetable factory, which cost 1.2 million Sudanese Pounds, was in production since 1968 with a capacity of 2,400 tons. It was due for rehabilitation just before the recent outbreak of the civil war. A grant of 8 million Sudanese Pounds had already been provided by USSR for this project which did not take off, and the fund is now being used to pay the wages of the factory's employee at the rate of 56,000 Sudanese Pounds a month. Another project whose execution was held up under the present circumstance is the Malut Sugar Factory. It was supposed to start in 1977 with a capacity to produce 110,000 tons of sugar with a cost of approximately US$ 85 million. Most of the equipment did not reach the project site and the cost of this non-existing project is 2.25 million Sudanese Pounds per annum paid as wages for a labour force that has not been given a chance to work. Wau Beer Factory was about to start production in 1983 when the law prohibiting alcohol production was passed by the Sudanese president as part of the Islamic *Sharia Laws* in 1983. The project, which cost 158 million Belgium Francs and 705,000 Sudanese Pounds, was left idle and paying an annual salary of 720,000 Sudanese Pounds to its work force. It is reported to have suffered damages due to the recent SPLA attacks in the area.

Effects of War on the State Budget

It is obvious that revenue collecting has halted in the war zone with serious consequences on social services and economic activity in the Southern regions. An analysis of the state's budget, as such, cannot explain the overall impact of the war on the central government's transactions, nor on the performances of different sectors of the economy. But, it can be useful in pointing to shifts in the destinations of expenditure and in the sources of revenue, and whether those shifts are direct or indirect results of the war. Moreover, it helps to identify how much certain sectors of the society, including the military, reap from the central government revenue in order to be able to execute their responsibilities amid the calamity of war. In this sense, the relationship between the military and society can be seen in terms of competition for public finance regardless of whether or not they share the same sentiments and politico-ideological commitment to the war.

In the Sudan case, taxes had normally contributed about 70 percent of the total revenue, but due to the imposition of the Islamic *Sharia Laws* in 1983 and the introduction of *Zakat* (Islamic wealth tax), the Government was not able to operate an effective tax system. This coincided with the beginning of the war in 1983 which interrupted and eventually halted tax collection in the Southern regions. From then on the Southern regions have been completely dependent on grants from the central Government finance but making no contribution to the national treasury. Although it cannot be documented an increasing war effort has meant that financial resources have been shifted from civilian to military purposes. Table 18 shows public sector finance operations 1983–1986. At least three observations can be made:

First, public sector overall deficit increased from 752 mn. Sudanese Pounds in 1983 to 2,747.1 mn. Sudanese Pounds in 1986/1987. This is coupled with an increase in defence and security expenditure by over 100 percent, i.e. from 260.6 mn. Sudanese Pounds to 650.0 mn., thus surpassing the total expenditure on economic and social services combined (587.4 mn. Sudanese Pounds) in 1986/1987. Second, public sector finance which had still been dependent on external loans and grants, became more dependent on domestic borrowing. Borrowing from the Bank of the Sudan rose to 1,525.1 bn Sudanese Pounds relative to an external finance of 1,222.0 bn. in 1986/1987. There

Table 18. *Public Sector Finance 1983–1986/87 (in Sudanese Pounds mn.)*

	1983/84	1984/85	1985/86	1986/87
Central Government Revenue	1469.00	1485.50	1790.40	2741.80
Direct Taxes	404.50	300.50	351.60	407.20
Indirect Taxes	839.90	984.60	1222.60	1357.50
Other	224.60	215.40	216.20	977.10
Central Government Expenditure	1642.70	2512.20	3378.30	4287.00
Economic Services	74.30	196.00	208.00	313.00
Social Services	69.90	160.80	182.00	274.40
Loan Repayments	212.00	118.00	465.40	474.40
Defence and Security	260.60	462.00	473.10	650.00
Local Government	270.30	360.50	557.00	1003.30
Other	755.60	1214.90	1492.80	1571.90
Current Surplus or Surplus (net)	–173.60	–1026.70	–1587.90	–1545.20
Development Expenditure	483.00	453.00	369.10	1179.90
Agricultural Sector	135.40	139.10	69.30	274.80
Industrial Sector	119.20	110.10	74.60	285.50
Transport and Communication	67.60	52.10	57.90	224.50
Service Sector	59.40	54.30	32.50	111.00
Other	101.40	97.40	107.80	282.40
Public Entities Position with the Banking System	892.63	411.95	887.10	1071.40
Sudan Gezira Board	144.38	127.07	287.90	359.20
Centr. Electr. and Water Corp	10.23	4.15	23.50	20.60
Sudan Railways	51.85	19.89	19.20	25.10
Other	686.17	260.84	556.50	666.50
Public Sector Overall Position	–753.90	–1543.50	–2026.50	–2747.10
Financing of Deficits	753.90	1543.50	2026.50	2747.10
External Loans	571.20	869.70	1213.20	1222.00
Banking Financing (net)	182.70	673.80	813.30	1525.00

Source: Ministry of Finance 1983–87

is no reason to attribute dependence on national borrowing to any sign of economic recovery or the Governments orientation towards self-reliance. It is largely due to the Government failure to reach an agreement with the IMF since 1986. The decline in external borrowing is largely a result of financial embargoes and the unfavourable position of the Sudan with international creditors. Third, current central Government deficit increased from 173.7 bn. Sudanese Pounds to 1,026.7 bn, 158.9 bn and 1,545.2 bn in 1983, 1984, 1985, and 1986/1987, respectively. When development expenditure and public entities are calculated, the public sector overall position shows a deficit of 753.9 bn. Sudanese Pounds, 1,543.5 bn., 2,026.5 bn. and 2,747.1 bn. in 1983, 1984, 1985, and 1986/1987, respectively.

The details of this larger synthesis can be coloured with more details to examine the proportion of defence and security expenditure during peace and war. Table 19 shows some of the basic differences in the structure of central government expenditure during peace and war. The main features of the table can be summarized as follows:

First, defence and security expenditure rose from 9 percent of the total Government expenditure in 1981 and 1982 to between 14 percent to 18 percent for the period from 1983 to 1986/1987, i.e. during the war.

Second, defence and security expenditure eclipsed loan repayments in 1983, 1984, and 1986. In other words, defence began to take priority over arrears payments which, we presume, has prompted the position taken by the IMF and the suspension of further loans to the Sudan.

Third, the only explanation for the increase in expenditure on social and economic services relative to the period before the war, is the general orientation of the economy towards services financed by grants from the NGOs in the form of relief and medical supplies for the displaced and the destitutes.

Therefore, war began to claim a substantial share of the central Government expenditure and the re-orientation of funds from social development to defence and security. In fact, the ultimatum which the senior military officers issued in February 1989 (four months before the June coup) demanded either an increase in military finance to enable the army to fight the war or that the Government should ensure the peace agreement between the Democratic Unionist Party (DUP) and the SPLA.

The Impact of War on Balance of Payments

This section explores the balance of payments with a keen eye on the impacts of war on economic activity. In a situation of a worsened external balance and a financial resource gap of 15 percent, falling exports at a rate of 8–12 percent of the GDP, an uncertain overall export price outlook, and declining real producer prices for major agricultural

Table 19. *Defence Expenditure as % of Total Government Expenditure 1980–1986/87 (in mn. Sudanese Pounds)*

	1981	%	1982	%	1983	%	1984	%	1985	%	1986	%
Defence and Security	65.10	9.30	108.50	9.50	260.60	15.80	462.00	18.30	473.10	14.00	650.00	15.10
Economic Services	34.30	3.00	66.30	3.00	74.30	4.50	196.00	7.80	208.00	6.00	313.00	7.30
Social Services	29.90	4.20	55.60	4.90	69.90	4.20	160.80	6.40	182.00	5.30	274.40	6.40
Loan Repayments	106.90	15.30	217.90	19.20	212.00	12.90	118.00	4.70	465.40	17.80	474.40	11.00
Local Government	256.10	36.60	352.90	31.10	270.30	16.50	360.50	14.30	557.00	16.50	1003.30	23.40
Others	207.20	29.60	333.40	29.40	755.60	46.00	1214.90	48.40	1492.80	44.20	1571.90	36.70
Total	699.50		1134.60		1642.70		2512.20		3378.30		4287.00	

Source: *Economic Survey, Ministry of Finance 1980-86; Bank of Sudan 1987*

crops; any attempt to study the war as the sole contributor or explanation of the economic crisis is unrealistic. However the war, as explained earlier, is one of the major contributors to the crisis and can therefore be added to the above factors but with extreme caution.

According to the World Bank (1985: 62), "public deficit and foreign financing rose sharply up to 1981/82, while both public and private sector savings fell. Because the public sector commonly financed expenditures by borrowing from the Bank of the Sudan (printing money), rather than mobilising resources from the private sector through taxation and appropriate pricing policies, domestic inflation became a major problem, and the country faced a severe external debt crisis". The situation changed to the worse after the beginning of the war in 1983. Central Government finance has already been dealt with in the previous section. Here we are most concerned with national savings and investment during 1980–1987, making the basic assumption that the war must have directly or indirectly contributed to low savings and investment. Three major characteristics emerge with respect to savings and investment (World Bank, 1985; Ministry of Finance, 1990).

First, the decline in both national and domestic savings were accompanied by increased reliance on foreign resource mobilisation until 1985. However, as stated earlier, since 1986/1987 (and for the first time) borrowing from domestic sources has surpassed foreign resource mobilisation.

Second, there is an obvious decline in gross savings and investment when measured as a percentage of current GDP. Sudan in 1982/1983 reached a paradoxical situation whereby the current account deficit reached an unsustainable level of 16 percent of the GDP, while its natural option of depending on foreign borrowing was blocked by it's worsened record of human rights violations since 1983. This left little or no option other than excessive domestic borrowing with far reaching consequences on the economy in general.

Third, low savings alone are not the sole factor inhibiting investment, since it is assumed that the war effort, high debt service ratio to the GDP and exports all affect saving levels as well as investment.

Balance of payments is another important indicator of the manner in which the overall structure of the economy operated before and during the war.

Of particular interest to the discussion on the economic impacts of war is whether the country is in a financial position to shift resources from the productive sectors and social welfare or to borrow from the domestic or foreign sources in order to finance the war. In a crisis situation such as that of the Sudan, continuous balance of payments deficits, and dependence on external sources for arms deliveries can only add to the crisis. In both ways, it means the shift of financial resources from financing the basic needs of the population to the war effort which in turn entails the destruction of the already meagre infrastructure in the war zone. These we believe have aggravated the already desperate situation of the balance of payments and the national account in particular.

The Hidden Economy

For ideological and political reasons no Government would reveal the manner in which war is weakening its economic social and political structures. The economy of war is always hidden and only very scanty official references as to how much it costs can ever be made available. Grave as the economic impact of the war has been the picture we have painted so far is incomplete, because it has made no mention of arms deliveries and the full thrust they have had on the economy. The data presented so far, I hold, has underestimated, real economic costs. Three factors have contributed to give us a reduced impression of defence expenditure, and have not been accounted for in the official statistics. These are:

First, the creation of tribal militias by the Popular Defence Act of 1989 to assist the armed forces in combating the SPLA. The tribal militias took over the role of the armed forces and hence relieved the Government from huge financial responsibilities. But this was done, with total disregard to the implications of this policy on inter-group relations in the future.

Second, was dependence on large quantities of free arms deliveries from the Middle East, especially Libya, Jordan and Iraq. According to the various reports, Sudan armed forces would have not been able to recapture many of the garrison towns which they lost to the SPLA without the intervention of Libya in the war since 1986.

Third, donations by the general public, businessmen and Sudanese emigrants in the oil-rich Arab countries, both in cash and kind. Estimates of these donations vary from 1 billion Sudanese Pounds in 1985 to 500 mn. in 1989.

On the other hand, arms imports constitute a large proportion of the Government budget, although little is disclosed to civilians and even to officials outside the military establishment. Table 20 shows Sudan imports of major weapons during the period of the first civil war (1955–1972), during peace (1973–1982) and the present war until 1986/1987. Arms imports have been high during peace as well as during war, which suggests that the armed forces were preparing for war anyway. Second, the arms accumulated during peace alleviated immediate pressures on the budget during the initial period of the war in 1983.

Table 20. *Value of Major Arms Imports (in $ mn. at constant 1985 price)*

	1955/1972	1973/1982	1983/1985
Total arms imports	452.0	451.0	119.0
Average per annum	26.59	50.1	39.7

Source: Arms Transfers to the Third World, 1971–1985: Michael Brzoska and Thomas Ohlson, Oxford University Press, 1987, appendix 6 a: Value of Imports of Major Weapons by the Third World, 1951–1970 and appendix 6 b: Value of Imports of Major Weapons by Third World, 1971–1985.

Table 21 shows the ratio of arms imports to total exports during 1981 to 1985/1986. The figures read as follows:

First, the high arms imports of 40.6 percent of total exports in 1981/1982 was a result of a series of mutinies of the Southern battalions which culminated in the 1982 resistance of soldiers in Kapoita, Melut, Rumbek and Juba to being transferred to the North.

Second, arms imports in 1984/1985 surpassed oil and petroleum imports and were certainly higher than medicine and chemicals or transport and equipment imports. However, the fact that arms imports do not usually appear in the official statistics obscures the analysis and questions the truthfulness of the methods applied in determining the performance of national account, foreign trade and balance of payments.

Third, years of decreased arms imports were usually followed by years of increased imports to compensate for weapons used and ammunition loss. This is known among the military as a "modernisation" process whereby new advanced weapon systems are introduced to replace the old ones.

The average arms imports from 1981 to 1985/1986 were $69.4 mn. per year compared with $628.6 mn. average for the imports for the same period. The average of the arms imports to total imports was 11.0 percent for the same period. Needless to say, since Sudan has experienced continuous deficit balance of trade, the percentage of arms imports to total exports is much higher.

In short, the general performance of the economy does not always reflect the full thrust of the impact of war. The hidden economy of the war is difficult to assess, but the scanty material available does not document accurately the substantial shift of central government finance from development and social welfare to military procurement and activity.

Table 21. *Major Weapon Imports as % of Total Export, 1981–1985/1986 (in $ mn) at Constant 1985 Price*

	1981	1982	1983	1984	1985/86
Value of major arms imports	141.0	87.0	11.0	87.0	21.0
Exports	346.0	606.8	893.5	463.5	833.2
As % of exports	40.7	14.3	1.2	18.8	25

Source: (1) Material compiled by author from M. Brzoska and T. Ohlson, op. cit., Arms Transfers to the Third World, 1987. (2) Bank of Sudan Reports, 1981–1986.

Economic Embargoes

Sudan failed to reach an agreement with the IMF in 1986 and the country was officially declared ineligible for further IMF borrowing. Sudan's inability to re-schedule its $12 billion debt by the end of 1989, was an obstacle to any settlement with other creditors. The failure to repay outstanding arrears of about $1.2 bn. by November 1989 made the Sudan an unfavourable recipient for external credits.

The present war exerted an enormous burden on Sudan economy and claimed vast financial resources which could have otherwise been used for development instead of destroying it. Two of Sudan's main suppliers of development assistance, USA and the EC, have introduced embargoes on the Sudan as a result of the war. The US State Department announced recently that a law passed in 1985 prohibits US aid to any regime that overthrows an elected government and does not return to civilian rule within six months. This has reduced the already reduced American aid to the Sudan. The European Parliament in June 13, 1990 passed a resolution urging the European Commission to suspend all aid programmes to the Sudan, to freeze scheduled discussions about the Lome Convention and to suspend considerations and implementation of all projects agreed upon under Lome II and Lome III which had not yet begun. These measures were sought in view of Sudan's violations of fundamental human rights and rejections of appeals for clemency for prisoners condemned to death following arbitrary and summary trials. However, humanitarian aid and relief operations have not been suspended either by the Americans or by EC. Sudan is increasingly dependent on the oil-rich Arab countries for external resources to finance an increasing deficit in the state budget and balance of payments. This we assume cannot compensate for shortages in capital goods, chemicals and equipment necessary for the agricultural and industrial sectors or the raw materials and spare parts the country needs to import from the industrially advanced countries.

An attempt has been made to highlight the impact of war on the state budget, balance of payments, the hidden economy and the economic embargoes imposed on the Sudan as a result of its involvement in this bloody war. It is clear that the impacts of war are pervasive and, as such, they penetrate directly or indirectly through all sectors of the economy. Although no definitive figure has been provided as to what the cost of the war is, several estimates put it at $2 mn. a day. We believe that this is a gross under-estimation, since such a figure would have cumulative consequences on other sectors of the economy as well. For example, hampering the government's ability to purchase raw materials and spare parts for industry or the maintenance of the agricultural sector which is the backbone of the economy. The human cost of war and its impact on society, and children especially, is not measurable.

Chapter 7

Effects of the Current War on the Southern Sudan Economy

Introduction

Wars are recurrent features in the history of Southern Sudan. Every one of them has contributed to the destruction of the few social and economic infrastructures that exist. Perhaps none has done this more than the current one (1983 to date).

This chapter attempts to highlight the impact of the present war on the economy of Southern Sudan. However, due to the difficulty in collecting data in Upper Nile and Bahr el Ghazal regions, the analysis is limited to Equatoria. It is assumed that despite the lack of data from those two regions the effects of the war on the economy in Equatoria are similar to those in the other two regions. The analysis covers the main sectors of the economy, i.e. agriculture, commerce, trade and industry and socio-economic development. The numerical data are based on the paper *"The Effects of the Current War on the Economy of Equatoria"*, written by the author, et al, in Juba, September, 1989 for presentation to the National Peace Committee.

Agricultural Sector

Food and Cash Crop Production

Despite the abundance of natural resources Southern Sudan imported much of its food from the North and Northern Upper Nile Region, especially sorghum the main staple food. Apart from the rail link to Wau and the seasonal road to Juba via Malakal, the bulk of this food was transported by steamers up the White Nile. They were halted in 1984 when the Sudan Peoples Liberation Army (SPLA) sunk a steamer just north of Bor. Since then no steamers have attempted to reach Juba from the North. Equatoria became practically isolated from the rest of the country except by air.

A positive outcome of the isolation of Equatoria is that people began to increase local production of food crops, especially the staples sorghum, maize and cassava. Both the Equatoria Regional Government and a number of agricultural development programmes and NGOs supplied the necessary farm inputs and trained manpower to help the small-holder farmers to produce surplus food crops. The most noticeable of these organisations are the Equatoria Regional Agricultural Programme (ERAP) and the Norwegian Church Aid, Equatoria Programme (NCA/EP). The increase in surplus food crop production compensated for the lack of imports from the North and, in fact, helped/necessitated the growth of co-operative movements for producers and the marketing of this surplus. Such was the abundance of surplus that Equatoria exported surplus food crops to Bahr el Ghazal Region and Jonglei Province of the Upper Nile Region.

As the war escalated in 1985/86, the SPLA began infiltrating into the productive areas in Equatoria resulting in the displacement of farmers from the rural areas to secure zones in the urban centres and the neighbouring countries. SPLA operations and the counter attacks by the national army led to the virtual closure of development projects in the Region with consequent disruption in the supply of the needed farm inputs and extension services.

The sharp fall in food crops production can be shown by the example of Yei and Kajo-Keji Area Councils, which are the most productive in Equatoria in terms of food crops.

Table 22. *Marketed Surplus of Food Crops in Yei and Kajo-Keji (Metric Tons)*

Crop	1984/85	1988/89
Dura	3,800	Nil
Maize	2,400	"
Cassava Flour	3,200	"
Groundnuts	200	"
Millet	300	"
Beans	150	"
TOTAL	10,050	

Table 23. *Cash Crop Production and Livestock Population 1984/85 and Today*

Harvested cashcrop/live-stock population	1984/85	Expected prod. /population for 1988/89	Present situation
coffee	6,000 mn. tons	7,500 mn. tons	1,500 mn. tons
tea	200 mn. tons	700 mn. units	Nil
tobacco	60 mn. tons	1,000 mn. units	Nil
cattle	1.0 mn.	1.2 mn.	0.75 mn.
sheep	1.5 mn.	1.8 mn.	0.80 mn.
goats	0.5 mn.	0.8 mn.	0.20 mn.

Clearly, the war had completely wiped out the total of 10,050 metric tons of marketed food surplus, by 1988/89. As a consequence, the dependence of the urban and displaced population on relief food increased.

The Forestry Sub-Sector

Given the necessary inputs and conditions conducive to production the forestry sub-sector could contribute substantially to the economic and social development of Equatoria Region. The sub-sector is a major source of public revenue and contributes both directly and indirectly to employment. Through its influences on micro-climatic conditions it enhances agricultural productivity. The forests also provide browse from shrubs and trees which constitute up to 30 percent of animal feed and the ecological niches necessary for the different animal species. Last but not least the forests provide the bulk of energy needs and contribute in many other ways to welfare. The Forestry sub-sector in the Region is made up mainly of sawmilling or the production aspect of the forestry. Up to 1984/85 Equatoria operated a total of nine sawmills with a total production of sawn timber of 5,750 cubic metric tons valued at over 3 million Sudanese Pounds. Concern with the environmental aspects of forestry have been recent. The following table shows the position of forestry production.

Table 24. *Sawn Timber Production Equatoria Region. 1984/85 and 1985/86–1987/88*

Sawmill group	Production and value of production*				
	1984/85			1985/86–1987/88	
	No. of sawmills	Production M3	Value Sudanese Pounds	Production M3	Value Sudanese Pounds
Imatong group	2	4,000	2,401,200		
Loka group	6	500	158,900	555,6	176,570
Upper Talanga tea project	1	1,250	662,125		
All	9	5,750	3,222,223	555,6	176,570

*Cost M3 are respectively (in Sudanese Pounds) 6000.3, 317.8 and 529.7 for Imatong, Loka and Talanga Groups of mills.

From 1985 the security situation in Equatoria began to worsen leading to the conditions prevailing today. Not a single sawmill out of 9 operates now.

The impact of the war on the sawmilling industry in Equatoria has resulted not only in the loss of revenue but also in the loss of employment to many rural-based people. Even in the towns those whose livelihood depended on sawn timber, like carpenters, builders, wood-carvers etc. have been rendered redundant or under-employed. The sawmilling industry, until the current war, was a major provider of direct and indirect employment. Over half of the 1,573 employees of the sub-sector earned their living from sawmilling.

Other effects of the war on forestry production are related to loss of investment and the need to cover demand through importation of timber. Additional investment from the World Bank (in the case of the Imatong Group of Mills) and from the German Government (in the case of the Loka Group) was going to raise total timber production to 21,500 cubic metric tons by 1990. This is estimated to value (at 19484/85 prices). 10,752,450 Sudanese Pounds and constitutes about half the country's timber needs. These will now have to be imported.

In terms of forestry development, Equatoria has 33 forest reserves, 17 in Eastern and 16 in Western Equatoria Provinces. Only a handful of these remain in government-controlled parts in the west.

Although largely a plantation process, afforestation contributes to revenue generation in various ways, e.g. sale of products of thinning, land clearance. Table 25 shows the continuous drop in revenues from such products.

Table 25. *Production and Value of Some Forest Products in Equatoria Region. 1982/83–1984/85 and 1985/86–1987/88*

ITEM	1982/83		1983/84		1984/85		1985/86–1987/88	
	Qty**	Value	Qty	Value	Qty	Value	Qty	Value
Poles All	41061	266897	33784	219596	36502	237263	18407	704646
Fence posts (PCS)*	6699	43544	4957	32221	3961	25747	19920	129480
Shebas (PCS) at 3 Sudanese Pounds	5409	16227	660	1980	506	1518	NA	–
Bamboos bundles at 5 Sudanese Pounds	2474	12370	895	4475	1758	8790	1683	8415
Charcoal sacks 12 Sudanese Pounds	12	24	58	696	NA	–	319	3828
Firewood M^3 16 Sudanese Pounds	939	15024	958	15328	183	2928	68	1088
Total		354086		274296		276246		847457

*AV price/pole is 6.5 Sudanese Pounds
**Qty = Quantity

The present population of Juba is estimated to be half a million and the majority are displaced persons from the rural areas. This process of rural migrations into the remaining relatively safe towns for both food and security has had negative effects on the environment. Because relief support cannot meet all their needs, more and more people have taken to trading in forest products. There is a massive deforestation in and around Juba estimated to cover 30 square kilometres annually of cleared forests and bushes. This is desertification at its fastest and has obvious deleterious effects on agriculture and the environment. The situation is worsened by the price-incentives of trading in firewood and charcoal (about 300 Sudanese Pounds per bag in 1989). In addition, the cost of local building materials such as poles, shebas (types of poles), thatching grass, etc.. has also risen tremendously.

The Commercial, Trade and Industrial Sectors

Commercial Sub-Sector

Due to the war many government departmental activities have come to a standstill, amongst which are those of the Department of Commerce. This department controls and regulates all internal and border trade activities between neighbouring Zaire, Uganda and Kenya. The basis of the border trade lay in the importation of cement, iron sheets, petroleum products, and finished consumer goods. In return, Equatoria exported salted and sun-dried fish, salt to Zaire and soap to Uganda (the latter products being produced in Northern Sudan). In addition, there was an active re-export business in vehicles, radios, bicycles and textiles.
The Department of Commerce received its revenue from registration and license fees for both exporters and importers, business profit tax and surcharges for goods re-exported through Equatoria. This border trade flourished before the current war which has in effect led to the closure of all borders and thus stopping all commercial activities related to it and hampering internal trade as well. The following table depicts the general decline in revenue collection as the war intensified; as opposed to a gradual increase from 1974/75 onwards. An assessment of the supply of goods side also exemplifies the negative impact of the current war.

Table 26. *Revenues from Border Trade (in Sudanese Pounds)*

Year	1974/75	1975/76	1976/77	1977/78	1978/79	1979/80
Revenue	1,821	6,209	6,683	11,350	13,089	26,529
Year	1980/81	1981/82	1982/83	1983/84	1984/85	
Revenue		42,732	27,478	12,969	15,680	

N.B. The revenue covers the following:
i) Sale of import and export forms
ii) Registration of importers and exporters
iii) Registration of business names and partnerships, etc.

Unfortunately recorded data is almost impossible to come by, even for goods transported by steamers to Malakal and Juba. It can however be said safely that before the present war, the supply of goods to Equatoria was satisfactory and expanding, especially through border trade. As an example, see table below.

Table 27. *An average of the amounts of registered goods transported yearly between 1980 and 1988 at the Yei check-point.*

Item	Sugar	Cement	Wheat flour	Salt	Dura
Quantity	16,451	18,558	86,234	6,590	29,776

It is worthwhile noting that these are goods trucked via Yei to Juba from Kenya, Uganda, and Zaire. However, as mentioned earlier, all such flows of goods have stopped due to the war.

Fuel supply is an important item of the overall supply situation. The Ministry of Commerce and Supply in the defunct Southern Region, started a fuel supply project in 1977. The Petroleum General Administration (P.G.A.) carried out feasibility studies to establish fuel stations and depots in the main towns of the South. As a result, a number of stations and main depots in Juba and a store in Wau were established. The flow of fuel and other fuel products increased significantly between 1977 and the early 1980s as depicted by the figures below.

Table 28. *Flow of Fuel and Related Products (1977–early 1980s)*

Item	1977	1978	1979	1980	1981	Total
Petrol in drums	911	816	34,368	421	455	45,170
Diesel in drums	19,099	1,078	77,341	1,827	2,247	101,592

With the escalation of the war from 1983 up to the present there has been a sharp drop in the flow of fuel products to the Region as shown in Table 29.

The differences in the drop in fuel supplies as from the period 1977 to 1983 and from 1983 to 1988 are shown in Table 30. The negative consequence of the war on fuel supply and consumption in the Region has resulted in soaring of fuel prices in the black market. Secondly the lack of fuel in the region has retarded work in the government units particularly in the field of project implementation and supervision. Thirdly the shortage of fuel has resulted in shortages in the supply of water and electricity for domestic use in Juba Town.

Table 29. *Flow of Fuel (1983–1988)*

Item	1983	1984	1985	1986	1988	G/total
Petrol in drums	4,027	4,314	1,368	4,751	2,226	20,701
Diesel in drums	5,054	5,595	2,047	7,490	18,628	26,557

Table 30. *Differences between (28) and (29) above*

Item	1977–83	1983–88	1977–88	Difference
Petrol in drums	45,170	20,701	65,871	24,469
Diesel in drums	101,592	26,557	128,149	75,035

Prices

Prices have been rising steeply since 1983 due mainly to the following factors:

1. Tremendous rise in transportation charges.
2. Continued devaluation of the Sudanese Pound against the US Dollar.
3. Fall in the supply of local produce.
4. Absence or reduction of imports.

The impact of the above factors can be illustrated by the price indices of selected commodities taken at random from the period 1981–82 to 1988–89. Consider the table below (i.e. Table 31).

That table shows prices in real terms of some basic commodities in Juba Town. From the period 1981/82 to 1988/89 most commodity prices rose by about 20 times and over 30 times in the case of sugar. These were caused partly by the general inflation in the country, by frequent devaluations of the Sudanese Pound, but more by the high freight costs, especially charged by air cargoes, and the scarcity in the supply of many commodities.

Table 31. *Selected Commodities Price Indices*

		1981 to 1982				1988 to 1989			
S/ no.	Commodity	Retail price	Unit	Retail price	Unit	Retail price	Unit	Retail price	Unit
1.	Sugar 50 kgs (imp.)	39.50	bag	0.79	kg	1240.00	bag	24.80	kg
2.	" 50 kgs (Kenana)	30.61	"	0.60	"	751.19	"	15.00	"
3.	Petrol 200 l	103.50	drum	5.68	gallon	2306.27	drum	52.41	gallon
4.	Milk powder 400 gr			2.10	tin	900.00	carton	40.00	can
5.	Cement 50 kg (imp.)	–	–	21.73	bag	–	–	–	–
6.	Rice 45 kg	51.40	bag	1.02	kg	1118.00	bag	27.00	kg
7.	Dura (local)	27.56	"	3.67	kg	724.61	"	103.50	kg
8.	Wheat flour 50 kg (imp.)	28.80	"	0.45	kgs	559.46	"	11.25	kg
9.	Salt 50 kg	14.13	"	0.60	"	–	–	13.00	"
10.	Edible Oil	19.88	jerican	1.00	litre	414.00	jerican	13.00	litre
11.	Washing soap	8.10	carton	0.18	piece	187.95	carton	4.17	piece
12.	Onion	50.16	bag	0.25	tin	1300.00	bag	18.00	kg
13.	Tomato Paste	19.71	carton	0.25	tin	600.00	carton	6.60	can
14.	Domoria	477.71	bale	16.04	roll	4404.70	bale	293.65	roll
15.	Dry Cells	100.90	carton	0.35	pair	1450	carton	11.25	pair
16.	Kerosene	134.17	jerican	1.63	gallon	–	–	–	–
17.	Beef	–	–	0.54	kg	–	–	30.00	kg
18.	Mutton	–	–	0.66	"	–	–	30.00	"
19.	Meat weight /bones	–	–	0.40	"	–	–	25.00	"
20.	Gas Oil	–	–	–	–	2261.95	drum	51.51	gallon

Industry

As already discussed earlier, industrial development in Southern Sudan is almost non-existent. However, before the war a few light industrial ventures were operational in Juba Town; for example, a carbonated soft drinks factory, a small ice factory, an allied furniture mart, Haggar Cigarettes and Tobacco Factory, Juba Automatic Bakery, Panorama Slippers Factory and a score of elastic and leather works. The war has led to the closure of all these industrial ventures. Their owner/managers have fled, leaving their workers unemployed. The reasons are the by now familiar problems of high costs and/or lack of transport for fuel and raw materials and the insecure environment. The owners, who were mostly Northerners, considered the risks in operating even in Juba, too high. Perhaps needless to say, all other industrial undertakings in other towns or rural sites have stopped because of the war.

Socio-Economic Development

Successive Regional Governments have produced comprehensive development plans which all aimed to accelerate socio-economic development. But none yielded the desired results for reasons already discussed.

The development budget in the Region depends on resources from the Central Ministry of Finance. Since the first Southern Regional Government in 1972 up to the present time, the gap between the approved budget and the actual amount received hampered implementation of projects. Table 32 illustrates this gap.

The rigidity or outright unwillingness of the Central Ministry of Finance to release funds has always been a source of frustration to the Regional Ministers and their officials. Much time and money is spent in 'chasing' approved funds to be released in Khartoum. The arrival of 'the cheque' from Khartoum, whether for development projects or just salaries is received with relief by both the civil servants and the general public. But the story does not end there.

It is common knowledge that, especially in the case of development funds, diversion of funds (or even their embezzlement) eats the meagre resources that reach Juba. If not, why have old establishments that already had some existing structures, like the Nzara and Mongalla Agro-Industrial Complexes not taken off? Most Southerners born prior to or around 1940 certainly can remember the products they used to purchase from these two industries, e.g. soap, cooking oil, sugar, damurria (a type of cloth), etc. From the time of the 17 years War up to today these industries were never really revived and the present war has just killed what was already dying. The level of implementation of projects in the South was only 23.71 percent in 1974/75 and only rose to 60 percent in 1982/83. With the onset of the current war this must be closer to zero per cent, if anything. Even corporations which operate in Juba, like the Equatoria Development Corporation (EDC) and the Equatoria Trading Corporation (ETC), have been reduced to paying wages and salaries for virtually idle employees, let alone the waste of production capacities. Some of the causes of this low capacity utilisation are beyond the control of the management of the two corporations. Air freight per kilo between Khartoum and Juba is now over 10 Sudanese Pounds and that between Nairobi and Juba involves hard currency which the Region does not have.

Table 32. *Development Budget, 1974/75–1982/83*

Year	Approved Budget	Amount Received
1974/75	7,135,510	1,692,404
75/76	7,164,248	1,623,484
76/77	15,331,963	3,624,413
77/78	32,490,000	5,697,119
78/79	22,500,000	7,821,743
79/80	17,500,000	10,305,152
80/81	18,000,000	12,804,491
81/82	16,000,000	13,399,510
82/83	16,000,000	12,645,348

The private sector could play a role in enhancing socio-economic development, but as I mentioned above the *Jellaba* traders have historically been unwilling to invest their profits and savings in the South. The present war is an excuse to extort black market profits from the needy population in towns through unrestrained rises in prices. Reports from Juba indicate that merchants willingly air-freight goods from Khartoum to Juba where they can sell at 20 times or more than Khartoum prices. For example, a kilo of sugar costs 3 Sudanese Pounds in Khartoum while in Juba it is 60 Sudanese Pounds or above. Soap sells in Khartoum at 0.25 Sudanese Pounds to 5 Sudanese Pounds a piece depending on the quality and type; while in Juba where every type of soap is scarce, none sells at less than 2.50 Sudanese Pounds. The same pattern exists for all other commodities to the extent that very few parents in Juba buy sweets or biscuits for their kids.

A persistent problem in the economic development of Southern Sudan, therefore, is the absence of a significant local indigenous merchant or commercial class with sufficient capital for local investment. It is mainly for this reason that in 1985 the Equatoria Regional Government started a project for the establishment of Equatoria Commercial Bank (ECB). Broadly, ECB is to promote trade, commerce, industry and agriculture (to mention only a few areas of operation) in the South and of course the Sudan as a whole. It is to be a national bank but with a focus on Equatoria and the South as a whole. The Bank has been registered but has not started operating due to the war climate which discourages prospective shareholders from investing in it. The attempt however shows the need for the South to establish financial institutions which can mobilise the financial resources generated locally for re-investment and thus create opportunities for capital and financial formation. Only then can the private sector be said to be contributing effectively to the overall socio-economic development of the Region.

Not only has the war destroyed or rendered unusable the economic infrastructures in the South, but basic social services have been affected adversely, e.g. education, health and water services to cite the most important. Apparently all the rural primary, junior and secondary schools in the Eastern Bank of Eastern Equatoria Province and some parts of the Western side of the Region have stopped operating. The following table shows the status of schools for the whole of the Southern Sudan. An estimated total number of 6,226 pupils and students have reported to Juba in search of education. With the few educational facilities in Juba many of these children could not go to school, partly because some of the schools are occupied by displaced people and the capacities of the existing classrooms are limited. For instance, a normal classroom in Juba now has over 100 pupils/students. Unfortunately such conditions of overcrowding make it difficult for teachers to control and follow each student's performance, guaranteeing a high rate of failure. It is also equally important to note here that over 90 percent of school age children of all levels of education in the entire Region are going without education.

With the influx of displaced citizens from the rural areas of the Region to the major towns of Juba, Yei, Maridi, Yambio, etc. the health facilities in these towns cannot provide the necessary services i.e. the drugs, equipment, doctors, etc. Poor sanitary conditions and high rate of malnutrition have been continuously causing high infant as well as adult mortality rates. Presently Juba a population of has approximately

500,000 people, with a doctor/patient ratio of 1:43,400. Certainly, even in any normal situation where there are all necessary facilities, drugs, etc., sufficient and effective services cannot be provided with only eleven doctors in such a big town. Among the Juba population there is a sizeable population of partially or permanently disabled persons caused either by anti-personnel mine explosions or received in battle cross-fire. This class of citizens require special social services, such as provision of artificial limbs. In general, lack of adequate health services can only aggravate the situation with more death from diseases, malnutrition, etc.

Table 33. *The Status of Primary Schools in Southern Sudan (By Region)*

Region	Open	%	Closed	%	Total
Upper Nile	8	3	249	97	257
Bahr el Ghazal	16	5	339	95	355
Equatoria	150	28	389	72	539
Total	174	15	977	85	1151

Source: Ministry of Education, Khartoum, 1990

Table 34. *The Status of Junior Secondary Schools in Southern Sudan (By Region)*

Region	Open	%	Closed	%	Total
Upper Nile	4	8	45	92	49
Bahr el Ghazal	9	13	59	87	68
Equatoria	38	46	44	54	82
Total	51	27	148	73	189

Source: Ministry of Education, Khartoum, 1990

About 80 percent of the population of Equatoria Region live in the rural areas, where there is a general lack of clean drinking water. As a result of the scarcity of water, women and children spend a lot of their time fetching water over long distances from their homes. In some areas as many as six to ten hours are spent daily transporting water from far away sources for household use. Moreover, the quality of the water is poor, containing a number of water-borne diseases which claim many lives each year especially among the children. The same is occurring in displaced persons camps in the towns where the situation is worsened by lack of proper sanitational facilities.

Table 35. *The Status of Secondary Schools in Southern Sudan (By Region)*

Region	Open	%	Closed	%	Total
Upper Nile		0	13	100	13
Bahr el Ghazal	5	38	8	6	13
Equatoria	9	39	14	61	23
Total	14	28	35	72	49

Source: Ministry of Education, Khartoum, 1990

The Directorate of Rural Water Development is responsible for the development and supply of clean drinking water in Equatoria Region. Before the beginning of the current civil war it was drilling bore wells in the rural areas at the following production rates annually:

a) Cable tool rig 40 bore wells
b) Air drill rig 120 bore wells

In all, the Directorate and some international bilateral agencies and non-governmental agencies (NGOs) drilled 1,900 bore wells throughout Equatoria between 1974 and 1984.

The present war has adversely affected these operations. Drilling activities are now limited to urban areas like Juba, Maridi, Yambio and Tombura and in a much reduced intensity. The production rate has now fallen to:

a) Cable tool rig 10 bore wells per year
b) Air drill rig 30 bore wells per year

The water sources installed in the rural areas have been destroyed by the SPLA or the Army or have run into disuse because of lack of maintenance.

The withdrawal of the international bilateral agencies and NGOs has limited the ability of the Directorate of Rural Water Development to meet the increasing demand for clean drinking water in the urban centres and the few accessible rural areas. In addition, the Directorate now has to depend on funds from the National Corporation for the Development of Rural Water Resources (Khartoum) as decided in the

National Conference on Technologies in Rural Drinking Water, held in Khartoum from 10/10/87 to 13/10/87. This decision meant that funds were now subject to delays in their release from Khartoum and the Directorate officials spend more time in follow-ups there, whereas previously the funds were part of the Regional Development Budget in Juba and so easily released on demand.

As mentioned earlier the above analysis of the impact of the current war on Equatoria Region can be assumed to apply by and large to the situation in Bahr el Ghazal and the Upper Nile Regions. It is axiomatic therefore that the present war has resulted in the almost total destruction of the economic and social infrastructures that existed prior to its emergence. From the spark in Bor the war has now engulfed the whole Southern Sudan burning everything and everyone in its way. An old African saying aptly describes the aftermath of such wanton death and destruction:

> "When the banana dies—its children succeed it. But when the fire dies—it covers its face with ashes." [74]

Which case will apply to Southern Sudan, the banana's or that of the fire?

Footnotes and References

1 Lagu, J. *Decentralisation: A Necessity for the Southern Provinces of Sudan*, Sammar Printing Press, Khartoum, 1981.

2 Mills, L. R., (1976),*Population and Manpower in the Southern Sudan*, International Labour Organization, p. 138.

3 Mills, L. R. (1976), *ibid.*, p. 141.

4 Mills, L. R. (1976), *ibid.*, p. 142.

5 Garvey-Williams, F. A. and L. R. Mills, (1976), *Education in the Southern Sudan: The Educational System and the Prospects for its Development*, Juba.

6 Beshir, M. O. (1968), *The Southern Sudan—Background to the Conflict*, C. Hurst and Co., London, p. 9.

7 Gray, R. *History of the Southern Sudan, Oxford University Press*, 1961, p. 79.

8 Gray, R. *ibid.*, p. 78.

9 Hurst, H. E. (1952), *The Nile: A general Account of the River and the Utilisation of its Waters*, London, Constable.

10 Sanderson, G. N. (1965), *England, Europe and the Upper Nile*, Edinburgh University Press, pp. 6–7.

11 See Gray, R. (1961), *op.cit.*, pp. 58–69, for an account of the slave trade which took place in Bahr el Ghazal, 1857–69.

12 Holt, P. M. (1962), *A Modern History of the Sudan*, Weidenfeld and Nicholson, London, p. 69.

13 13. Holt, P. M. (1962), *The Mahdist State in the Sudan, 1881–1898*, Oxford.

14 Collins, R. O. (1962), *The Southern Sudan, 1883–1898, A Struggle for Control*, Yale University Press.

15 Collins, R. O. (1962), *ibid.*, p. 57.

16 Gray, R. (1961), *op.cit.*

17 Collins, R. O (1971), *Land Beyond the Rivers*, Yale University Press, New Haven, p. 324.

18 Collins, R. O. (1971), *op.cit.*, p. 325.

19 Holt, P. M. (1958), *op.cit.*, has described the incident at length and so we need not recount it here except briefly.

20 Collins, R. O. (1971), *op.cit.*, p. 328.

21 Collins, R. O. (1971), *op.cit.*, p. 335.

22 Collins, R. O. (1971), *op.cit.*, p. 335.

23 Collins, R. O. (1971), *op.cit.*, p. 336.

24 Collins, R. O. (1971), *op.cit.*, p.337.

25 Albino, O. (1970), *The Sudan: A Southern View Point*, Oxford University Press, London.
26 Statement by H. A. MacMichael (then Civil Secretary of Sudan) quoted by Collins, in Diamond and Burke (eds.) (1966), *The Transformation of East Africa*, N.Y., pp. 375–76.
27 Beshir, M. O. (1968), *op.cit.*; Abbas, M., (1951), *The Sudan Question*, Faber and Faber Ltd., London; Abdel Rahim, M. A. (1958), Ph.D. Thesis submitted at the University of Manchester in 1958; and many others.
28 Alier, A. "The Southern Question", in Wai, D. M. (ed.) (1973), *The Southern Sudan: The Problem of National Integration*, Frank Cass, London.
29 Beshir, Abbas, Abdel Rahim, *op.cit.*
30 Wai, D. M., (1973), *op.cit.*, Appendix VII.
31 "Report of the Commission of Enquiry into the Torit Mutiny, 1956", contains details of the events that took place and its causes.
32 Samuel M. Makinda (1987), "Sudan: Old Wine in New Bottles", *ORBIS, A Journal of World Affairs*, summer, p. 223.
33 Manifesto of the SPLM/SPLA, 1984.
34' Sudan Government (1954), *Jonglei Investigation Team, The Equatorial Nile Projects and its Effects in the Anglo-Egyptian Sudan*, Khartoum, p. 245.
35 Tothill, J. D. (ed.) (1948), "Agriculture in the Sudan", *Oxford University Press, London*, see particularly pp. 819–26 and pp. 888–918.
36 Tothill, J. D. (ed.), (1948), *ibid.*, p. 820.
37 Tothill, J. D. (ed.), (1948), *ibid.*, p. 821.
38 Tothill, J. D. (ed.), (1948), *ibid.*, p. 822.
39 Tothill, J. D. (ed.), (1948), *ibid.*, p. 892.
40 Tothill, J. D. (ed.), (1948), *ibid.*, p. 891.
41 Sudan Government (1955), *Southern Development Team, National Resources and Development Potential in the Southern Provinces of the Sudan: A Preliminary Report, 1954*, London, p. 100.
42 Tothill, J. D. (ed.) (1948), *op.cit.*, p. 819.
43 Beshir, M. O. (1968), *The Southern Sudan: Background to the Conflict*, C. Hurst and Co., London.
44 Tothill, J. D. (ed.) (1948), *op.cit.*, p. 916.
45 The figure of 1,500 tons of cloth annually imported is found in Tothill, J. D. (ed.) (1948), *op.cit.*, p. 916.
46 Tothill, J. D. (ed.) (1948), *op.cit.*, p. 918.
47 Reining, C. C. (1976), *The Zande Scheme: An Anthropological Case Study of Economic Development in Africa*, Northwestern University Press, Evanston, Ill.

48 Barnet, A. S. (1974), *Gezira and Zande: The Success and failure of Two Cotton Enterprises in the Sudan*, Occasional paper, University of East Anglia.

49 Southern Development Investigation Team (1955), "Report on Natural Resources and Development Potential of the Southern Provinces of the Sudan", Sudan Government.

50 Mills, L. R. (1976), *Classified Manpower in Agriculture in the Southern Sudan*, October, Juba.

51 Figures taken from the *Six-Year Plan for the South (1977/78–1982/83)*. See section on crop production projections.

52 Figures found in Mills, L. R. (1976) *op.cit.*.

53 Government of Sudan (1977), *Six-Year Plan of Social and Economic Development in the Southern Region*, Juba, June.

54 Figures obtained from L. R. Mills (1976), *op.cit.*

55 Government of Sudan (1977), *The National Six-Year Plan for Comprehensive Socio-Economic Development* (1977/78–1982/83), Khartoum.

56 Mills, L. R. (1976), *op.cit.*

57 "Economic Mission to the Southern region" (1973), International Bank for Reconstruction and Development, Nairobi.

58 JP15 = Joint Project No. 15.

59 Figures obtained from the "Six-Year Plan for the Social and Economic Development of the Southern Region", Juba, October, 1976.

60 Yor, A. Y. (1975), *An Analysis of the Anzara Factory*, unpublished B.Sc. dissertation, University of Khartoum.

61 Regional Ministry of Agriculture (1981) "A Progress Report on the Mongalla Agro-Industrial Complex", June, Juba.

62 "Programme of Action for the 4th Regional Government of the Southern Provinces", Juba, July, 1982, p. 3.

63 Regional Ministry of Information and Culture (1977), "Peace and Progress", Juba.

64 Statement by one of the most prominent of the Northern traders in Juba, May, 1981.

65 Figures found in the section on power in the main document of the Six-Year Plan for the Southern Region (1977/78–1982/83).

66 Beshir, M. O. (1977), *Educational Policy and the Employment Problem in the Sudan*, Development Studies and Research Centre, University of Khartoum, Monograph Series, No. 3, Khartoum, May. This study does not have enough comparative data on South versus North.

67 Government of Sudan (1981), "Annual Budget Speech" by the then Regional Minister of Finance, Regional Ministry of Finance and Economic Planning, Juba.
68 Beshir, M. O. (1977), *op.cit.*, p. 33.
69 IBRD (1973), "Report of a Special Mission on the Economic Development of Southern Sudan", Country Programmes Dept. 1, Eastern Africa.
70 Wai, D. (ed.) (1973), *op.cit.*. See Appendix of this book.
71 Government of Sudan (1977), "The Six-Year Plan of Economic and Social Development, Southern Region (1977/78–1982/83)", Regional Government, Juba, June.
72 Six-Year Plan, *ibid.*, Chapter IV, 4.1.
73 Six-Year Plan, *ibid.*, Chapter IV, 4.2.
74 Obotunde Ijimere (1982), *The Imprisonment of Obatala,*, Heineman, London, p. 58.

Kolibri 360 GmbH
Ferdinand-Jühlke-Straße 7
99095 Erfurt, Deutschland
produktsicherheit@kolibri360.de